NORTHERN APPALACHIA REVIEW

VOLUME 4

CATAMOUNT
PRESS

an imprint of Sunbury Press, Inc.
Mechanicsburg, PA USA

an imprint of Sunbury Press, Inc.
Mechanicsburg, PA USA

For information about special discounts for bulk purchases, please contact Sunbury Press Orders Dept. at (855) 338-8359 or orders@sunburypress.com.

To request one of our authors for speaking engagements or book signings, please contact Sunbury Press Publicity Dept. at publicity@sunburypress.com.

FIRST CATAMOUNT PRESS EDITION: February 2023

Set in Adobe Garamond.

Publisher's Cataloging-in-Publication Data
Names: PJ Piccirillo, et al.
Title: Northern Appalachia Review Volume 4.
Description: First trade paperback edition. | Mechanicsburg, PA : Catamount Press, 2023.
Summary: An academic literary journal focused on writers from the northern Appalachia region.
Identifiers: ISBN : 979-8-88819-048-7 (softcover) | ISBN : 979-8-88819-049-4 (ePub)
Subjects: FICTION / Anthologies | LITERARY COLLECTIONS / American / General | FICTION / Cultural Heritage.

Product of the United States of America
0 1 1 2 3 5 8 13 21 34 55

Continue the Enlightenment!

Northern Appalachia Review

Editor-in-Chief and Founding Editor: PJ Piccirillo

Nonfiction Editor: Rita Wilson
Fiction Editor: Virginia Rafferty
Poetry Editor: William Scott Hanna
Editor, Book Reviews, Interviews, and Literature of the Outdoors and Environment: Dominique Hoche
Copy Editor: Debra Reynolds
Managing Editor: Samantha Backstrom
Assistant Poetry Editor: Kathleen S. Burgess

Fiction Readers
Nicole Ravas
Debra Reynolds
Arthur Turfa

Poetry Readers
Kathleen S. Burgess
Mark Saba
Matthew Vargo

Nonfiction Readers
Nicole Ravas
Debra Reynolds

Cover Art: Mark Saba
Cover Designer: Lawrence Knorr
Book Designer: Crystal Devine

Advisory Board
Brad Barkley
Bonnie Culver
Gerry LaFemina
Nancy McKinley
David Poyer

The Northern Appalachia Review publishes once annually. U.S. subscription rate is $20 for one copy. See submissions guidelines at NorthernAppReview.com. Address all correspondence to The Editors, generalinquiries@NorthernAppReview.com.

C O N T E N T S

KEY:

F—Fiction

NF—Non-Fiction

P—Poetry

L—Literature of the Outdoors and Environment

I—Interview

INTRODUCTION

Thank you for furthering our mission to seek and share literature that speaks to the unique web of communities and landscapes, commonalities and conflicts, we call northern Appalachia.

Over the past four years, the staff of the *Northern Appalachia Review* have had the honor of hosting the work of 110 poets, essayists, and fiction writers, ranging from first-time authors to poet laureates, including several we have nominated for the Pushcart Prize and The Best American Essays.

The 216 works of prose, poetry, interviews, and reviews populating our four volumes mark the first collection of literature to finally contemplate the essence of our special parcel of America.

We're proudest that our authors, in reaching out with their art and sharing our sense of purpose, have represented every crevice and corner of northern Appalachia. One of those contributors, Mark Saba, has become a team member. Mark is not only a Swiss Army knife of literature, having published fiction, nonfiction, and poetry, he has a background in graphic design. For our back cover, Mark conveys the network of voices that composes this edition.

What you don't see represented by Mark's pushpins are authors tied to but living outside our region: Williamsburg, Kentucky; Saline, Michigan; Bethesda and Bowie, Maryland; Charlottesville, Virginia; Knoxville, Tennessee; New York, New York; Belmont, Massachusetts; Missoula, Montana.

Northern Appalachia may be finite in its geography, but the impressions this place has on its people stay with them no matter where they journey.

Thank you, readers and contributors, for making the Northern Appalachia Review the premier literary journal of its region.

PJ Piccirillo
Founding Editor
Editor-in-Chief

Clara, Never Married

The pack of young ruffians swarmed around her, circling, whooping, jostling her wagon, a raucous boys' chorus chanting the same old silly taunt:

Clara, Clara, never married,
Had a beau she bled and buried!

She lashed out with her pocketbook, grazing one, the Stormer boy, the only one she recognized. Another looked familiar, a Wonderling maybe; he might have been among the mourners when John Jacob Wonderling was laid out in their parlor last week. They ran off, Clara giving chase. The Wonderling boy was littler than the others, slower. She caught him, clutching the scruff of his neck—his accomplices skipping merrily away, laughing, unconcerned about whatever ill fate might await their companion. Clara reached rudely down the back of the boy's knickers, seizing the top of his underpants, yanking hard. The little boy levitated with a yelp. Satisfied by the sight of him hobbling away, crying, tugging at his crotch and hiney, Clara turned back toward her little red wagon and the dead dog she was hauling.

Little hooligans! What was the world coming to when a body couldn't pull her wagon down her own Main Street without risking life and limb? She noticed Mr. Sandt standing in the doorway of his drug store, shaking his head. Shaking his head! Never mind raising a finger toward the boys. Never mind raising a voice.

"Boys will be boys," he said, stepping back inside.

Across the street, Hannah Haines, walking by on her way to the bank, glanced down at her gloves, pretending she hadn't seen Clara and the whooping, hollering pack of wild Indians that nobody in their right mind could have missed. Well, that suited Clara just fine. Old classmates they might be, but they hadn't really shared a civil word since seventh grade. "Hannah!" she yelled, "Hannah Haines!" and stuck out her tongue, but Hannah Haines never turned her head, never batted an eye.

Clara took up the wagon handle, chin up, shoulders back, and resumed pulling the rattling contraption and its dog meat cargo over the rough patch of sidewalk in front of Mason the lawyer's. She was headed toward her place, Smyers Funeral Parlor, at the other end of Main. A block and a half down, past the courthouse, she spotted the man they called Squirrel—she'd know his lurch, the broom in his hand, from a mile away. The boys spotted him at the same time and raced across the street, cutting in front of Mr. Schwab's gig. His pony shied up and he pulled on the reins and took a swipe at the ruffians with his whip, to no effect, and soon the boys were swarming around Squirrel like a whirlwind in a cornfield, taunting him, hollering, poking, and pushing. Squirrel took a clumsy swipe or two with his broom only to have one of the boys snatch it from his hands. Off they ran again, whooping and hollering all the more, waving the broom in the air like a scalp they'd just taken. Mr. Schwab climbed out of his gig to give chase with his whip, but the boys had already disappeared around the corner of Coal Alley.

Mr. Schwab climbed back into his gig. Squirrel walked on, faster than before. Clara tugged her wagon across Pershing, passing under the shadow of the tall, stately courthouse. Her neighbors went about their business, a man in a fancy suit and bowler ascending the courthouse steps, Mr. Clover smoking his pipe on the porch of his general store, two men coming out of Clarkey's Restaurant, picking their teeth and chattering, and half a dozen other folks standing, strolling, laughing, admiring the early morning sky overhead. All of them had witnessed the boys' antics; none had lifted a finger. Boys will be boys. None had come to Squirrel's aid—Mr. Schwab had been roused to action not by the boys' attack on the gimpy little man, but by his own close encounter—and none had come to hers. And the boys. They'd raced by all the others, dodging, swerving out of their way to avoid them. Clara paused, squeezing the handle of the wagon. Why? Why had the pack of ruffians set upon no one else but her and Squirrel?

She had a face suited to puzzling, her shiny, wide brow tapering down to a pointy, hooked chin, and when she set her features to concentrate, it was like a wedge splitting the task in two. Deep in thought, she resumed her journey once more, hauling the dog, oblivious to the bumps and rattles and stares, contemplating, deciding finally that the common bond she shared with Squirrel was this: formidability. She and Squirrel, with their wagon and broom, were the only two formidable targets on the street. Their formidability stemmed, of course, from opposite poles: She was a capable, imposing young lady, apprenticed to a dark profession that most folks feared, while Squirrel was an enigma of unknown origin who also inspired fear, fear of a different color—the fear of ending up like him. Until now, Clara had felt nothing more than scorn and perhaps a modicum of pity for the ubiquitous little man—he daily trekked the length and breadth of Main Street before disappearing into his obscure den, wherever it may be, each night—but now she felt a distant kinship.

When she came to the corner of Coal Alley she turned, and sure enough, as she suspected, she found Squirrel's broom in a patch of over-grown dead weeds, right where the little hoodlums had flung it. She retrieved it, laying it by the dead dog, its handle poking stiffly out past the end of her wagon beside the dead, drooping tail. A large brown mongrel, the dog had apparently thought it would be a good idea to chase away an automobile—a menacing new presence on the streets of Hartsgrove—but had fared poorly in the encounter. It was a short-hair, not too badly damaged, perfect for her plan.

Clara determined to return the broom to its rightful owner. Squirrel's sole means of livelihood was sweeping this floor and that, this patch of sidewalk and that, for whatever charity the owners might give him in return. She felt for the gimpy little man.

Reaching her house, she slowed. She lived with her father above their funeral home—*Smyers Funeral Parlor*—a somber, dark green building of clapboards and shingles, fancy crowns over the windows, an ornate cornice below the flat roof. The porch was an unholy mess, all torn apart, under repair because of a bad infection of dry rot. One last glance down Main—no sign of Squirrel. Above the courthouse, a morning cloud was infused with a pleasant pink color, a color that put her in mind of her formaldehyde solution.

She wheeled the dead dog through the laurel bushes down the little walkway by the house as quietly as she could. Stealth was paramount. Evasion of her father was entirely necessary if her plan was to succeed. She parked the wagon by the door to her prep room. Carrying the dog inside, placing it on her embalming table, she fetched a bucket of water back outside to clean out the bed of the wagon. When she returned, broom in hand, she heard footsteps on the stairway, her heart sinking.

He must have spied her through the window. He sometimes seemed omniscient.

Her father. The door opened, and there he was, arms folded over his chest. He stared at Clara from beneath the brim of his top hat. He was a small man, shorter than his daughter, but his stature did nothing to diminish his presence. "Clara," he said, sternly.

Perry Barnett watched his mother failing, getting feebler by the day, and the more she failed, the more he began to resent his wife, Marjorie, who seemed indifferent to the old lady's suffering. For a while, he'd tolerated it—he understood that his mother's complaints, her indulgence in self-pity, might be enough to try the patience of a preacher—but when Marjorie said she wanted his mother out of their house, that was when she crossed the line.

"Whatever happened to the milk of human kindness?" he said.

"She's been milking and milking and milking," Marjorie replied. "I'm about dry."

Marjorie was a woman with a hard stare, and she used every ounce of it on Perry. She was standing by the door, impatient; she'd never been late for work a day in her life, and she didn't intend to start now. She'd had to wake him up—he stood in his nightshirt by the bedroom door— to tell him there was no reason on God's green earth why his mother couldn't get along just fine up at the Memorial Home. Heaven knows their house was small enough to begin with, and she wanted her parlor back—the room where Perry'd put in a bed and installed his mother when she was too far gone to live on her own. Marjorie worked as a domestic for the Darlings—she was wearing her gray uniform, white cuffs, collar, and apron—and Perry suspected her employment there was the seed of Marjorie's discontent. He suspected the Darlings' mansion, their opulence in general, had wormed a hole in Marjorie's heart.

He lowered his voice. The parlor door was closed, but the walls were thin. "You know she ain't going to be around that much longer. Why can't you just wait?"

"That one thrives on misery. Why, she'll probably outlive the both of us." Marjorie sniffed, opened the door, and was gone.

Perry shook his head. He was a man with lazy brown eyes and a wart on his cheek, built like a scarecrow and blessed with a similar disposition, easy going. His wife's no-nonsense attitude, her straightforward approach, was one of the reasons he'd hitched up with her in the first place. He'd always been content to let her handle the bother of the family purse strings, to argue with the neighbor when his rooster kept shitting on their stoop, let her be the one to take the little bird with the broken wing—the one their son, Donnie, had found in the yard one day when he was a youngster—and put it out of its misery. But lately he'd taken to wondering if it wasn't all coming back to bite him in the britches.

Mother was awake, out of her bed and sitting in the wingback chair—Reverend Packard's favorite place to park his fat ass when the room was still a parlor. She'd made a nest of pillows and blankets, her yarn and darning, old socks and sweaters and mittens she was mending—or trying to. Her thick old fingers no longer worked the way they used to.

"Next week I'll be sixty-six years of age," she said with a mixture of pride and dread. She looked at her hand scritching the heap of yarn and clothing as though it were a kitten. "Just think of the thousands of stitches I've stitched."

"Wished I had a nickel for every one," Perry said. He walked to the window, pulled open the curtains, let the light in.

"If wishes was fishes," she said.

"What would you like for your birthday, Mama?"

"A big thick slice of Ella John's bread and butter. I got so hungry for a slice of her bread and butter I couldn't hardly sleep at all. It's the hardest thing to want and can't get."

Ella John was long dead, as his mother well knew. "Maybe we can get you somebody else's bread and butter that's just as good."

"Maybe I won't be around for my birthday," she said. She breathed in the sick air of the room and let it out again. Her hair was gray and snarled, unattended to, her face flushed and swollen, making her button nose even less substantial. Her legs and feet were more bloated than ever, red as red flannel. She began to cry. Again. Hardly a day went by without Mama tears.

Perry fixed his mother's breakfast—oatmeal and biscuits, none of Ella John's bread and butter to be found—and filled a tub with hot water to soak her feet, but she could do so for only a minute or two. It hurt so, she said. They tried the new ointment, but she was skeptical; she'd had her fill of doctoring. Nine different doctors in three years and not a one of them had done her a particle of good, she said; salves and ointments and washes and poultices to high heaven, and not a one of them had done her a particle of good either.

"What else can I do, Mama?"

"You can let me get back home."

"Your home's gone now. You know that. This here's your home now."

"Well Marjorie sure don't think so."

"Marjorie can be a little hard sometimes."

"No milk of human kindness, that's what her problem is."

Perry looked up, eyebrows aloft. "You could hear us?"

"These walls is thin as the icing she puts on her cake."

"She don't mean nothing by it."

"Who you trying to fool? Course she does. She resents me. She don't like having to care for me. She don't like that she's got to examine my rear end every night for carbuncles."

Another hoisting of the eyebrows. "Your rear end? Every night?"

"Sometimes twice. When I ask her to, she ain't quite hard enough to turn me down. Not when I cry a little too."

"Why, I didn't even know you had any carbuncles on your rear end."

"Oh, I don't," his mother said. Then she gave a hiccup of sorts, a hiccup Perry soon realized was something else, a failed attempt to stifle a giggle. "You ought to see the look on that woman's face every time she has to stick her nose down there and examine my hiney! Like she's fixing to bite into a big old sour lemon!"

Perry slapped his thigh, joining his mother's laughter, the hardest they'd laughed together in years. He laughed at the joke, at the look—he could see it plain as day—on Marjorie's severe face, at having his mother back, the mother he remembered, if only for the moment.

Withering beneath her father's glare, Clara felt her face burning. Without another word she gathered the dog up, carried it outside and dropped it back in the wagon.

Inside, she found her father waiting, sitting calmly on the embalming table where the dog had been, his legs crossed at the knees, hands clasped together upon them. "I've been told it isn't proper for a man to sit like this," he said, "with his legs crossed at his knees. It is a lady-like posture, they say, too feminine." Clara said nothing, blinking. "'How would you have me sit?' I always ask them. 'Like this?' At that her father uncrossed his legs, splaying his knees far apart. "'Is this manly enough for you?' I ask them."

Clara did not feel called upon to respond.

"My point, darling daughter, is this." He hopped down from the table, standing over the drain in the floor. "People have some very peculiar notions about what is proper and what is not. You cannot hope to educate ignorant minds, and there are probably none more ignorant than those that inhabit this little town. These are the same minds that will feel it is a matter of sacrilege for a funeral home to be undertaking its business on carrion. They will not want their dearly departed to be laid out on a table that has recently been home to buzzard bait. Do you follow my meaning?"

"I do, papa. But may I ask a question?"

"Of course, darling daughter."

"Who would know?"

"Who would know?'"

"Yes. Who. If I were to practice my craft on a dead dog, or, for that matter, on a dead groundhog, possum or piglet, who would know? There are no windows to peek in. No one would venture down here, ever, unless they were dead. It's the last place in the world anyone wants to be caught alive."

He set his jaw, refocusing his glare. "Word would get out. It always does." Then, when she said nothing, he said, "You didn't kill it, did you?"

"*No.* It was already dead." *This time,* she thought, but didn't add aloud.

"Good. At least there's that. So your intention was to practice your skills?"

"I need to work with the new tools." She nodded toward the shiny silver instruments arrayed on the table by the formalin bottles. "The hand pump in particular. I find it awful stiff and hard to use."

"You'll have occasion to use them soon enough. On a proper, human, specimen."

"But practice makes perfect, Papa. You taught me that. I really want to be the best mortician I can be. I want to make you proud of me."

"The trade isn't learned overnight. It's an art. Slow and steady wins the race."

She smiled her shy, icy smile. "Yes, Papa."

He nodded toward the broom leaning by the door. "Where did that come from?"

She told him what had happened, the pack of young hooligans setting upon Squirrel, her rescue of the broom, her intent to return it to its rightful owner.

"No," he said, wagging a finger. "Stay away from that—that man, that . . . whatever he is. He may be feeble-minded, but he is a male animal, with all the instincts of any male animal, regardless of species. I have heard stories. I have heard that he has, on innumerable occasions, exposed himself, for example. You are to go nowhere near him, for you are an attractive young lady, and the temptation might prove . . ."

Her face flushed. A tall and lanky girl with broad shoulders and an abhorrence of cosmetics—perhaps a result of the cosmetics she applied to her clients—she questioned whether or not she was attractive and wondered if her papa truly believed she was. "Yes, Papa."

"There's my girl." He made for the door, hesitating at the bottom of the stairs. "*Has* there been a groundhog? Or possum? Or piglet?"

Clara only smiled, her shy, icy smile.

Her father wagged his head. "As for the poor dog," he said, "dispose of it properly. Perhaps back where you found it in case someone is looking for their pet."

Returning to the wagon, Clara cocked her head at the dead dog. Its eyes were puckered shut as if it were sleeping a troubled sleep. She wheeled it farther down the path, past the stable, onto the alley that ran parallel to Main, and down to the pens behind Scheafnocker's butcher shop where the hogs snorted in the slop and mud. Gently, as if to not awaken it, she picked up the dog and carefully dropped it into the pen for the hogs to devour.

When Perry finally stepped outside, tears of laughter lingering in his eyes, he nearly tripped over the little man huddled on his stoop. "Jesus, Squirrel, I purt near stepped on you—what are you doing here?"

"Just setting," said Squirrel.

"Why didn't you knock?"

A little shrug like a hiccup. Knocking wouldn't have occurred to him.

Perry considered Earl Fawcett—his real name—to be a lost soul, a lost soul no one was looking for. He'd taken him under his wing mostly out of pity, he supposed. Squirrel trudged the length and breadth of Main Street and beyond, carrying his trusty broom for sweeping whatever someone might ask him to sweep for a penny or two. Often as not, when he wasn't sweeping or walking with his curious, lurching gait from an injury or ailment of unknown origin, he was dodging sticks or rocks or insults, whatever debris might be hurled at him by young ruffians, or by old ruffians—old, drunken ruffians—or those simply not pleased by the presence of a ragged little man in a smoky, tattered wool coat and dirty sheepskin cap.

They set off, Perry going slower than usual, Squirrel lurching along-side him. Perry said, "Where's your broom at?"

"I dunno, Perry. Some young fellas took it off me."

"Why would they go and do that?"

"I dunno. Maybe they needed a broom."

"Little hooligans."

"I guess they didn't have a broom."

"Let's go find it. How you going to make a living without your broom?"

"I dunno."

"We'll take a look," Perry said. "Maybe meantime you can help me out some." He was rebuilding the front porch of Smyers Funeral Home down on Main, repairing the dry rot.

Squirrel perked up at that. "I can hold the other end of the twine. I can sweep up your sawdust from when you saw."

"How you going to sweep up any sawdust without any broom?"

"Oh. Yeah."

They had to stop on the corner of Rebecca and East Main to let an automobile go by, climbing the hill in all its grumbling, backfiring, smelly glory. Perry found the sight maddening. It had gotten to where there were damn near as many automobiles as buggies, and he could taste the foul breath of them in the air, long after they'd passed by.

"Get a horse!" yelled Squirrel, a taunt he'd borrowed from Perry. Pleased with himself, he smiled at the taller man, his teeth the color of scorched linen.

They started up the little hill toward Main Street proper, passing the Baptist Church. "Where'd they snatch your broom at?" Perry asked.

"Up there," said Squirrel, pointing, "up there by Coal Alley."

They poked around the alley a while, all through the bushes near the old icehouse, in the barrels by Wilson's print shop, and along the banks overgrown with dead weeds. No sign of the broom. Perry was wondering how much a new broom ran for, but he couldn't picture Squirrel toting a brand-new broom around, not with those hooligans still on the loose. "I tell you what," he said. "My mama had a broom, all broke in and good and sturdy, and she ain't going to be using it anymore. I'll see if I can find out what become of it."

Squirrel took that under consideration.

As they headed toward Smyers Funeral Home on Main, the sun at their backs, Perry watched their shadows stretching out before them, leading the way, his long lanky shadow, the stubby one right beside it. "You should of seen my mama, the way she worried that broom," he said. "When she was sweeping out a corner, you'd of thought there was snake curled up in there she was trying to poke to death. She took dirt personal." Squirrel, trudging along just behind him, was quiet.

Perry said, "Her sweeping days is over and done with, I'm afraid. Poor Mama. She was a big lady to begin with, and now this dropsy, or whatever the heck it is—can't get any two doctors to agree on the time of day, let alone what's ailing mama—it's got her legs and her feet all swole up twice the size they ought to be. And she's in a fair amount of pain. God love her. I'm fearing the worst. I'm sure going to miss my mama after she's gone."

Squirrel didn't say anything. Perry thought he saw the shadow beside him shrink a little bit, and he realized what he was going on about. Here he was, jabbering on about his mama and her broom, and here was poor Squirrel, trudging along beside him with no place to go, without either a broom or a mama to call his own.

"Come on," Perry said, "let's go see about that dry rot up on Smyers."

Clara headed down Main, walking east, the sun on her face making it difficult to see down the street. Pedestrians were little more than walking shadows, but she could easily see that Squirrel was not among them. She'd encountered him on Main tens, maybe hundreds, of times, though, to the best of her recollection, she'd never exchanged a word with the odd little man. She thought surely he would have resumed his daily trek by now, but such was not the case. It occurred to her that with no broom he had little reason to return.

She saw Harriet Barnes, another old classmate, walking across the street by the American Hotel, holding hands with her mother, chatting gaily. A flare of anger shot through Clara. She stared, trying to decide if Harriet was doing it on purpose, intentionally rubbing Clara's nose in it. Clara's own mother disappeared, run off when she was two, abandoning her and her papa. And though Clara held no sentimental thoughts toward her mother whatsoever—she had managed just fine without her, thank you—some of her erstwhile classmates, Bucktooth Barnes among them, seemed to view Clara's motherlessness as another of her failures, like arithmetic. They assumed her mother must have had a good reason for deserting her.

She watched Harriet Barnes and her mother go into the American Hotel, without so much as a glance in Clara's direction. Fine. Clara stuck out her tongue in their general direction.

She stepped into Clover's general store. She'd often seen Squirrel sweeping his porch. Mr. Clover was standing behind his counter weighing penny candy, several large jars gaping open before him with big, hungry mouths. Clara asked if he might have any idea where Squirrel Fawcett might be found. She had his stolen broom and wished to return it to him.

"That pack of brats again?" said Mr. Clover. "They torment that poor little fella something awful. Course, they ain't the only ones."

"I found where they flung it, but he'd already taken off."

"Far as I know, he lives in his little shack somewhere over by the railyard, but I doubt you want to go traipsing the whole way over there."

"I'll traipse if I must," she said. "The fresh air will do me good."

"Yes," he said. "I should think so." His nose gave a little twitch, the sort of twitch she'd seen often, and she knew he was imagining the smell of her embalming room—as folks so often seemed to do.

Imagining Mr. Clover imagining her embalming room put Clara in mind of it herself. He was a tall, rangy man, Mr. Clover, white bib apron over his flannel shirt and blue jeans, wire spectacles and thinning hair running straight back over his head. The veins in his neck—these always caught her attention—stood out like ropes. She imagined him at rest on her table, as sooner or later she imagined just about everyone she encountered. She imagined slipping the needle into his carotid, the pump in her hand, the formalin flowing in through the arterial tube. She pictured the blood draining from his leg, swirling into the drain in the floor.

She imagined the other: the fluid engorging his visceral appendage.

A common phenomenon. The first time she'd seen it on her table— though not the first time she'd seen the male member in its inflated state—was on the body of a young farmer who'd been dragged to his death by a runaway horse. The part had magically swollen, arising like a cobra in the jungle, and had refused to lay back down again, as, she was to learn, they normally do. Her father went about her training only slightly perturbed, ignoring his daughter's blushes, explaining that in such instances there was a simple precaution against unwanted distraction among the loved ones at the viewing: He simply tied it down to the young man's leg with a piece of twine.

"You all right, Clara?" Mr. Clover said. "You look a little bit flushed."

"Flushed?" she said. "Oh, no, not me."

She left Mr. Clover with a frown on his face, stepping back into the sunshine of Main Street, trying to decide whether to traipse on over to the railyard or not. As she stood fretting, she saw, serendipitously, Perry Barnett coming down the street toward her. Beside him, lurching along, trying to keep pace, was Squirrel Fawcett. Delighted, she hurried off down the street to beat them to her home, which she knew to be their destination.

Lewie Smyers was an odd duck in his own right, as far as Perry Barnett was concerned. A smallish man, a pot-bellied imp, he'd grown bald over the years and compensated by letting what remained of his hair prosper and grow down over his ears in fringes that touched his collar. And by wearing a squat and dusty top hat. He usually wore the rest of his uniform as well, not only for services but for normal, everyday commerce: drab trousers and jacket and waistcoat of muslin. His horses, for hauling his hearse, he draped with fancy white lace spreads and tassels.

Perry didn't much care for the man—he saw something mean and slippery when he looked him in the eye—but a job was a job.

Squirrel waited outside by the torn-up porch while Perry went in to fetch his tools. He'd left them in the foyer, on the thick, quieting carpet. The windows were high, black gauzy drapes keeping the rooms in shadow. On his way back out, he bumped into Smyers, who seemed to have materialized—Perry hadn't heard a peep—top hat, string tie and all. "Morning, Mr. Smyers," he said.

"You working another job?" Smyers said.

"How could I be working another job? My tools is all up here."

"Where have you been all morning?"

"I got a sickly mother I'm taking care of," Perry said. "You know that."

"And I got a sickly porch. It'd sure be nice if people could walk in here without worrying about falling clean through and breaking a leg."

"Your porch'll get done. I brought along a helper today."

"Oh? I ain't paying you any more."

"I ain't asking you to. We set a price. A deal's a deal."

"Good," Smyers said. "The sooner the better. Appearances mean a lot in this business. No one's going to want their dearly departed's last hours above the dirt to be in a place with a tore-up, half-rotted porch on it."

Perry nodded. "I aim to have it done by the end of the week."

"Good." He clapped the taller man on the back, walking with him toward the door, adding on a lighter note, "We got to get that porch fixed up good and solid before we bring your mama in—that's one big lady."

Perry stopped, shaking Smyers' arm off his shoulder. "You know, Smyers, you got about as much sense as a shithouse snake."

"What?" Smyers said, a serious knot on his brow. "You told me yourself your mama's not long for this world. And that poor woman's so big, I don't know if I'm going to be able to fit her inside my hearse—I might have to use my wagon."

Perry hitched up his tool belt and headed outside, Smyers trailing behind. "What makes you think I'd bring her up here anyways?" Perry said. "Up to a place with a damned old rotted porch on it?"

Squirrel looked up from the stack of two-by-fours where he was hunkered.

"What the hell's he doing here?" Smyers said.

"He's my helper," said Perry.

"Not on my property he's not—get on out of here! Scat! Go on!" Shooing, he rushed toward the bewildered Squirrel, who made it to his feet just as Smyers arrived, pushing him hard.

"Now hold on!" said Perry.

Smyers shoved him again, Squirrel lurching away awkwardly down the street as fast as his stubby legs could stumble. He stopped at a safe distance, standing, facing away, his head down and his shoulders hunched up, as though weathering a hailstorm. "I don't want that creepy little retard anywhere near here," Smyers said.

"He's my helper," Perry said. "You want your porch to get done or not?"

Smyers looked meanly at Perry and pointed toward Squirrel. "I got a daughter in here—I don't want him nowhere near her. Who knows what all that pervert's been up to. There's been somebody creeping around here nights peeping in windows, and a lot of folks saying it's him."

Perry yelled, "Squirrel! Hey Squirrel! You been peeping in any windows lately?"

Squirrel took off running down the street, a shuffling, rolling gait.

"Now look what you done," Perry said. They watched Squirrel hightailing it. "He ain't been peeping in any windows. Hell, he's afraid of the dark."

He heard a noise behind him. Clara stood in the doorway, peeking out. Her wide brow glowed with excitement, her narrow lips pursed in bemusement. She was watching the goings-on with what appeared to be a curious apprehension, a curious delight.

An hour passed, then another. Clara busied herself in the kitchen, puttering, cleaning, keeping busy, replenishing the ice in the ice box, slicing the fresh loaf of bread, preparing her father's lunch, waiting for him to leave. Sporadic sounds of hammering and sawing came from the porch where Perry worked alone. Squirrel had not returned. Her father was keeping watch.

Later, before he left to visit his friend and bosom companion, Dr. Hickey, he instructed her to maintain vigilance, to be alert for signs of a trespassing Squirrel.

She assured him she would. She watched him leave on foot, Dr. Hickey's house being only down Main and up Pershing a block or so. When he was safely gone, she went out to the porch and watched Perry at his work for a while, his measured pace.

After a while she said, "Where do you suppose Squirrel got off to?"

Perry looked up, reached for his bandana, mopped his face. "Heck," he said, "he's probably up street somewheres ravishing some poor helpless woman."

Clara contained a giggle, though she couldn't stop the smile.

"I seen him once or twice down by the creek at Pershing bridge," Perry said, "maybe he's there. He likes to sit on the rocks and watch the water go by. Seems to put him in a trance almost, the way rubbing a frog's belly does."

That was where she found him. He flinched but didn't turn around when she called his name. He was staring at the water rollicking over the rocks.

"Squirrel," she called again. "I got your broom. You want your broom back?"

As soon as the words were past her lips, he was up, stumbling up the bank toward her, looking down. When he got there, he looked first at her feet, then slowly up as far as her hands. "Where's my broom at?"

"Back at my place."

She led him down the alley below Main, past the hogs' pens full of snorting beasts—a hank or two of dog fur was all that remained of her specimen—in through the back of her house to the prep room in the basement.

Her father should be gone for a good, long while yet. He and Dr. Hickey often spent hours over tea and coffee, brandy and cigars, resolving the problems of the world, the war in Europe, conscription and all its attendant unrest, the merits of the automobile versus the buggy.

Reunited with his broom, Squirrel grabbed it quickly and turned to go. "Squirrel," she said, two slow rolling syllables.

He turned with a blink and a frown, a blush overcoming his face.

"Aren't you going to say thank you?"

"Thank you." He reached for the doorknob.

"Hold on. Come over here. I got something to show you."

She had nothing to show him, nothing in particular. He was hers. She felt a sense of possession. There'd never been another living, breathing man in this room other than her father, who didn't count. From above, through the house, the muffled thuds of Perry's hammering sounded like a pulse. "Do you know what this is?" she asked Squirrel. "This is the table where I lay out dead people and fix them up to get buried."

Squirrel came to. His eyes were bright with color, hazel, that surprised her.

"What do you do to them dead people?"

She showed him the jugs of formalin, told him she pumped it into dead people to keep their bodies the way they were so the people who loved them could remember them that way, and not have to see them starting to rot. She showed him all the tools lined up in a row—how very shiny—and she took her mouth-closer and showed him which end went into his nose and which under his chin before she screwed it closed to shut the mouth. She put it up to his face to show him, but Squirrel giggled and squirmed away. She told him how the bodies sometimes twitched even though they were dead—couldn't he just imagine how that would make you jump?

"Do you want to play a pretend game?" she said.

His face opened up. "What kind of a game?"

"Here," she said, "hop up on the table. Wait—take your coat off first—we don't want to get the sheet all dirty." He hesitated, then started to take off his coat. She didn't know whether his hesitation was reluctance or mere gawkiness. She was at a loss too as to whether Squirrel wanted to play a pretend game, or simply didn't know how to say no. He stood next to the table looking at her, his face halfway between a grin and outright panic, his eyes both fearful and imploring. "Actually," she said, "your trousers are every bit as dirty as your coat."

In the quiet, the pulse of Perry's hammer from up above was felt more than heard, throbbing in Clara's temples, out to her fingertips. With a glance and a nod, she urged Squirrel's uncomprehending hands toward the knot of the twine that held up his pants. His dark red face was perplexed, his eyes a silent plea. "I won't *do* anything to you," she explained.

A sudden crash, the door bursting open.

Her father. A garbled bellow, the fringes of his hair in flight, his face red as raw meat under the brim of his top hat that went flying from his head as he rushed toward Squirrel. Squirrel scrambled around the table, ear lugs on his sheepskin cap flapping this way and that in panic, Clara crying out, Squirrel screaming. Two, three times around the table till finally her father, blind with rage, leaped across, seizing Squirrel by the shirt that seemed to disintegrate. He pummeled him, blow after blow, beating, kicking, thumps and cries and yelps, Clara's among them, her pleas lost in the tumult.

Perry looked up from his hammer at Clara screaming in the doorway. "Come quick! Come quick! Squirrel! Papa!"

Squirrel was on his back on the floor by the drain, flailing, emitting an animal wail. Her father had him pinned to the floor with one arm, the other arm stabbing, the scalpel in his hand flashing, slashing, bright blood erupting, splashing from the front of Squirrel's pants where Smyers stabbed and stabbed.

Perry's hammer was still in his hand. One swing and the scalpel was stilled. Smyers lay twitching on the floor beside the screaming Squirrel.

He carried him to Doc Shaffer's four doors down and left him. Squirrel had turned white, no easy feat given his dusky veneer; he was conscious, moaning. Perry figured he'd make it. Doc said he'd patch him up, get him to the hospital. Perry didn't wait around, not knowing when the law might turn up. He didn't know what damage he'd done to Smyers. He'd seen him move, he thought he'd recover as well, but he couldn't be sure. A hammer to the head, who could tell? So much he didn't know. He didn't know where to turn. He turned toward home.

Marjorie wasn't there. Late again. She seemed to linger at the Darling's longer and longer every evening.

His mother was alone in her room. It was nearly dark. The air was fetid, the awful scent of feces. He turned on the lamp, saw her, then turned it off again just as quickly.

Sitting so still, he could tell she was gone.

He staggered back to the bed and collapsed. It was a while before words came, his heart rampaging through him. His eyes grew used to the dark. He studied his mama, her head settled back on the wide wingback chair in her nest of blankets and knitting and darning, her eyes closed, at peace. It looked as though she'd scarcely moved all day.

He pulled over the little stool, sat close, took her hand. It was not yet cold.

"I'm sorry, Mama. I'm so sorry." Of course it was his fault. For what he'd done. He sat quiet for a while, looking at his mother's dark face. "I must look a sight, Mama, all this blood. Ain't none of it mine, though. I just walloped Lewie Smyers with my hammer."

His mama's hand twitched and Perry nearly shot through the roof.

"You done what?" she said, a groggy whisper.

"Dang, Mama!" said Perry. "I thought you was . . . I thought you was . . ."

"I ain't dead yet. I did shit myself though."

"So I smell."

"Setting here all the live-long day. Couldn't get up to make it in time. Couldn't even get up to get a glass of water. You done what to Lewie Smyers?"

"Walloped him on the noggin with my hammer."

"Good. Good for you. Maybe knock some sense into that little nincompoop."

"Maybe. But I doubt it. Lost my job, though, that's for sure."

"Could you get me a glass of water?"

"Sure, Mama. Want me to get you changed too? Least I can do. You used to change my dirty pants for me all the time when I was a little snot."

"Yes—my how the tide has turned," his mama said. "Ain't that the way of life?"

Then she took a contented breath and squeezed her son's hand. She smiled a tortured little smile. "But I'm thinking maybe we could leave that there chore for Marjorie?"

Clara was not surprised by how light her father was—or by how strong she was—lifting him onto her table. The hammering still throbbed in her temples even though Perry was gone. She undressed him, an awful, bloody mess, and carried his clothes upstairs and put them in the hamper, careful the blood didn't drip. When folks came in to view their loved ones, what would they think if there was blood all over the carpet? His top hat, unblemished, she returned to the hatbox on the chest in his room. She went back downstairs to prepare him. She supposed she should feel sadder than she did—for she did feel sorrow, she was certain it was sorrow she felt—but her father had taught her how to be quit of your feelings toward the one on your table, to just do the best job you can for them and for their loved ones.

He twitched once or twice. She flinched. But he'd taught her well. The twitches she ignored. The moans too. The moans she attributed to gas escaping. And even when it almost seemed as though he was breathing, she decided it could only be her wishful thinking playing tricks on her. The puttering of the lips, the murmuring sounds so nearly like his voice were so fragile and imaginary she decided she heard nothing at all.

The incisions she made were good and clean. He'd taught her well. It was a trade that would sustain her after he was gone, he'd said. The arterial and drain tubes went in easy as you please, and there were only a couple of clots that needed broken up. She worked the pump smoothly—she could scarcely feel it in her hand—and she watched in wonder as the fluid worked its magic on the cobra in the jungle. It was not the first time she'd seen the male member in its inflated state. She reached for the twine to tie it down, and the blood flowed out, down the tube, swirling pretty as a poem into the drain on the floor, and the rhyme bubbled up, and she hummed it to herself,

Clara, Clara,
never married,
had a beau she
bled and buried.

DNA

His father was firewood
His mother the ax.
He knows how to burn.

His grandfather was a porch
His grandmother a bicycle.
When he rests, he still moves.

His uncle is a lilac
Another a fence post.
He has boundaries around his blooms.

His brother is a leaf
His sister the sky.
He picks up the fallen in the open.

His father was a moon
His mother a hawk.
He hunts at night.

His grandfather was a trail
His grandmother a boot.
He travels light, and fast.

His uncle is a hemlock
Another a spade.
He is green and planted.

His brother is tea
His sister breakfast.
He prepares his own meals.

His father was grass
His mother a scythe.
He has been cut down.

His father was a sparrow
His mother a jay.
He is a flock.

His blood is a river.
He has readied his raft.

Huck and Jim

At the edge of a stream I mistake for a river, slender trees are rising
  like reeds and ripples are signifying and testifying.
    I think, therefore I say, "Huck and Jim,"

feeling an emotional cascade—a rush of joy for their life on the raft,
  a hopeful thing, a world of peace with nature and each other
    floating past the racial sickness on the shore,

a rush of grief for George Floyd, the four horsemen of the apocalypse
  bent on their sins of commission and omission. I pivot
    from the water to a path shaded by honeysuckle,

thick, leaning in, nectar hidden inside yellow flowers fluttering
  like birds. The multitudes by law enforcement murdered,
    say their names, have caused waves of grief, resistance

in a nation sick with the pandemic, yes, but also weariness
  of separation from each other. Huck and Jim,
    let us take crisp leaves from your book,

melt them in our mouths, and swallow them so that we might assimilate
  your amity and river grace. Huck, you had to fight for revelation.
    Jim, you always knew. Help heal us, you two.

Appalachian Holler Song

After a line by Thomas Hardy

Woman much missed, how you call to me, call to me,
howling like the Plott who lost the bear in the laurel,
and I, forgetting what hollow I walk, cross the stream
and crawl on hands and knees, re-spooling
the notes back to your throat
and the calling, calling.

Recall the Stuffed Bear

Recall the stuffed bear. And its ursine motif.
Its polyethylene-approximate black-black snout.
The wear on the feet from having been dragged.
A chalcedonic translucency to the banded glass

of the eyes: a reverence for blue afterimages,
the I-won't-ever-tell-on-you-kid dead centers.
It was my 4th bear buddy that year—1959—
since what 5-year-old has a sense of anything

except where the next hamburger and "Co-cola"
is coming from. Sometimes aren't we our parents
answering again their wants as a child? A child
with a memory as long as the thread-seam *T*

up and across the back of the bear. And even
the amnesiac leaving this one behind in the rain
in Whitesburg, Kentucky, a casualty somewhere
on the steps of the Letcher County Courthouse.

A taxi dropped my bear and me, and my granny.
Wasn't the August sky the color of a bad bruise?
Am I wrong to think she was hurrying me? After:
Where's your bear, Roy?—surely that child recalls

a Christmas-morning red-green necktie against
gray institutional walls, its plaid sweater vest
to anthropomorphize the threat of violence
and concomitant fierceness linked with bears.

My approximate pal had a name I shouted
as if calling the live thing to me. Its stitched
mouth, wire-curved ears—even loss was new
and seared you in the way it did back then.

Good Grief

O, January, limen, edge,
abiding at the limits of earth
and the extremity of heaven,
let us pass through your gates
unscathed and be borne again
into a new year!

Sun-blind face to eastern window
after days of overcast I sit as Janus
in this timeless not-season gazing
forward to light and inward to darkness . . .

Charlie Brown's voice has died of suicide.
His name was Peter Robbins, age 65.

We'd somehow travelled together my whole life,
he the noble sufferer, never aging, navigating
landscapes of childhood struggle and indignity.
What adults we saw were always only legs
or garbled voices, unintelligible authorities,

but the truth is this: he aged into a bipolar
schizophrenic addict real estate agent in
Van Nuys who served time for stalking
and threatening the plastic surgeon
who did ex-girlfriend's breast augmentation

and none of it was enough
or it was too much in the end.

I think of my own bipolar father
treading knife's edge brain chemistry
grasping rusted handrails of lithium
and Zoloft, my own tentative diagnosis
at 44 . . . my 17-year-old-son, in therapy,
telling us he hasn't slept much in days,
maybe weeks, so I sweep the mess from
his bed, put on fresh sheets, we climb
in bed together like we used to do.
The chronic insomniac will model
good sleep hygiene. Lights out.

I dream of Lucy, convincing Chuck
to trust her holding the football
one more time. "Hold it? Hah!
You'll pull it away and I'll land
flat on my back and kill myself,"
he says but starts his run-up nonetheless . . .

and every time she pulls that damned
pigskin away at the last moment . . .
Charlie's foot finds nothing, momentum
carries him spinning in circles up into the air . . .

I pull on sneakers, jog down frigid streets
hazed white with salt, squeezing briny drops
from stingy lachrymal bones, they fall and mingle
with the piles of old dirty snow glittering like piles
of diamonds someone swept up off the dance floor,

and Schroeder and Snoopy are jamming
on piano and bass, Linus and Sally
and the whole crew are there dancing,
but Charlie Brown is not there. . . .
He is still spinning through
the air out into the cosmos.

Impossible Loyalties

The rancid smell of scorched coffee wafted from the pot on the electric burner. I dumped the black sludge down the sink and dropped a slice of bread into the toaster. No butter, just a smidge of jelly left in the jar. The toast popped and I spread it with the jelly and laid it on the oilcloth where Mom sat at the table, the familiar aura of cigarette smoke signifying her outlook for the day. "You need something on your stomach," I said.

She slid the toast back to me. "So do you." She disappeared into the bathroom.

I stared at the toast, remembering the maxim we'd lived by most of the months Daddy had been gone: "Waste not, want not." One bite went down, and then another, but I couldn't trust a third, and no wonder. From the minute Mom's attorney had filed actions of nonsupport and mental cruelty, I'd tried to conjure a believable excuse to avoid the divorce hearing. At fourteen, I wouldn't be any help if things didn't go her way and she was too upset to drive home—lame. It was a school day, and I never missed school—still no good. And even though my stomach was regretting two bites of toast, claims of illness wouldn't relieve me of my duty. So there I was, down to the wire with no way out of playing Huckleberry.

March fog shrouded the Muskingum River, and the closer we got to Zanesville, the heavier the morning traffic and the more frazzled my nerves. My actual role in the proceedings was to wait on a bench outside the courtroom for the judge's decision. It wasn't the wait I dreaded; it was the decision. However it came down, I'd learned the day before, Mom and I couldn't both be winners; if she won, I lost. A big believer in telling the truth, Mom had felt compelled to inform me that if the divorce was granted, she and Daddy would share custodial rights. I was greeted with the news as soon as I cleared the door, stomping wet cinders from my shoe soles onto the mat.

"You can't be serious." The words came out sharper than I intended, but I didn't apologize; the cold, drizzly walk from the school bus stop had sabotaged any desire I might have had for niceties. "How long have you known?"

Mom was no good at hiding her feelings, and guilt flooded her expression just as the smoke from her cigarette clouded the space between us. "Long enough," she said, "but I didn't know how to tell you."

"You evidently found a way." I dumped my books on the table and unwound the plaid scarf from my neck. "How do 'custodial rights' work, exactly? He comes here, or I go to Wolf Creek?"

"I don't know." She dropped into a kitchen chair and tapped a long appendage of ash from her Kool, and even though I had a legitimate gripe, fear of coming across like Daddy and shaking her faith in my loyalty made me drop the sarcasm and the subject.

While I hadn't personally seen or heard all that my mother suffered at the hand of my father, her demeanor spoke to some instinctual part of my being, and I knew—I always knew—when there had been put-downs or the denial of needful things. The incident that goaded me the worst occurred not long before Daddy disappeared. A few weeks before, Daddy had the dentist replace several loose fillings for him. Only days later, when Mom's dental bridge broke, his response was a lift of the shoulders accompanied by "No money for teeth."

Seeing the look that passed between Mom and me, he attempted to justify the unjustifiable: "I am in the public eye where appearances matter." Once again, he had made clear Mom's position in his world.

Nearing thirteen, I hated him for his insensitivity and myself for cowardice. I should have pled her case with logos and pathos. That failing, I should have pitched the kind of fit that would force him to relent. Guilt plagued me every time I saw Mom stifle her smiles and shield conversations with her hand.

Thinking back, I am not sure Daddy was an intentional sadist, but he was wholly self-absorbed and believed the world owed him. As a young man, he'd had the desire to be a physician but lacked the financial means, so he settled for the barbering trade because of its affinity to medical practices in ages past. By the time he and Mom married, he had opened a shop in Duncan Falls, one of the smaller towns between Marietta and Zanesville. By the time I entered the picture, he was ranting against soot from smokestacks and the procession of coal and chip wood haulers grinding heavy truckloads to the Pig Iron and the Ohio Power plants across the river.

Daddy's idea of Utopia was living as his ancestors had deep in the hills of Washington County. Evoking rarely-outed courage, Mom had put her foot down. She was not leaving the relative convenience of Duncan Falls for the wilds of Wolf Creek, but she did concede to a day trip now and then. In my first memories of these, Daddy would hoist me onto his shoulders and walk the boundaries of the property, pointing out the foundation of the original dwelling and the quarry that supplied millstones for use in gristmills. The rustling of heavy overhead branches, the calling of birds, and the rush of creek waters transported him back in time. The original owner, a Scottish immigrant and builder of watermills, had succumbed to the lure of Wolf Creek long before Daddy.

Sometimes, it was well after dark before Mom's Chevy bounced back across the roadway toward civilization. By then, birds were nested in silent boughs, and the distant, strident engines of eighteen wheelers winding through the hills came to us in the evening damp. Passenger jets we hadn't noticed during the day invaded the night sky, their blinking red eyes competing for attention against ageless constellations. Looking back, I wonder if those intrusions of technology, rather than anything Mom said, were what angered Daddy on the return trip to Duncan Falls.

All I knew then was how I dreaded the ride home. Daddy would begin by holding forth on the primitive idyll. If Mom's opinion dissented, his rhetoric turned vitriolic and she ended up in tears. If I was lucky, I'd be asleep by then. If not, face buried in the aged upholstery, hands pressed against my ears, I simply endured.

Daddy's displeasure with Duncan Falls grew over the years. The spring I turned thirteen, he posted a "closed" sign on the barber shop door and moved to Wolf Creek by himself, just as if Mom and I didn't exist. By the end of November, we were out of coal for the furnace and the electric bill was overdue. Anything I'd earned babysitting had been swallowed up in school supplies. Even the account Mom had opened at the grocery store where she sometimes clerked was in arrears. The sympathetic owner filled page after page in our receipt book, marked each "Unpaid," and awaited a grand accounting—when and if Daddy ever showed up to pay. Shame and desperation finally drove Mom to desperate measures.

Of course, she picked a Saturday for the trip so you-know-who could go along as back-up. We left the curving highway just shy of Watertown and turned onto a gravel lane. Tall grasses swiped the sides of the Chevy as we advanced to a line fence and gate. I got out and lifted the loop of wire holding the gate closed and swung it open, flattening further the weeds in its radius. Mom pulled through and I replaced the wire. By the time I got back in the car my hands were numb with cold. Smoke a shade or two lighter than the brooding sky rose straight and steady above black treetops, marking our destination.

The gravel lane petered out into tire tracks and the land dropped toward a creek bordered by peeling sycamores, leafless strands of weeping willow, and moss-covered rocks. Flat steppingstones lay from bank to bank for dry weather crossing and a swinging footbridge hung a short way downstream for crossing during freshets. Mom pulled in beside Daddy's battered pickup, killed the engine, and reached for a cigarette.

We'd made it across the stones before the goats showed up, two spindly-legged curiosity seekers with chin-whiskers swishing in time to their busy jaws, pausing only to bleat a greeting. Mom stopped in her tracks, but as I advanced, the goats stepped aside, giving me a good looking-over through black, horizontal pupils. I touched the nearer shaggy head between its sloping horns. "See? They won't hurt you."

We climbed another slope to the house where Daddy's mother had been raised; its board and batten siding bore the gray patina of wood long unpainted. Stilts held the nearer part of the structure several feet off-ground while a foundation of cut stone anchored the rest. The goats returned to the open space under the house with its carpeting of straw as Mom and I took the curving uphill path to the door.

There, the sound of an ax splitting wood became audible. We entered a clearing among saplings where Daddy, stripped to his undershirt, turned tree limbs and trunks into sticks of firewood. His hair—normally combed straight back, emphasizing his widow's peak and high, prominent cheekbones—had fallen across his forehead. Only a day's growth of near-black beard had accumulated, suggesting to me that he had taken a job barbering in Beverly or Waterford, nearby towns.

He paused when we came into his line of vision and swung the ax one more time, driving its blade deep into the stump. He reached for the flannel shirt hanging on a shrub, his face glistening with a healthy skim of sweat, and used both hands to push back the unruly hair. Seeing that neither he nor I was going to break the stand-off, Mom said, "Hello, Francis."

"So you've spent yourself broke." He spoke without inflection, feigning nonchalance, but his expression, as he studied the changes that had come about in his daughter over the months, told a different story. Hair as dark as his was also pulled straight back, unveiling the widow's peak that had hidden behind bangs. A feminine version of the face he saw in the mirror had emerged during his absence. He let out a long-held breath and led the way back to the house.

Whether or not our likeness had struck Mom, all I saw in her face was anxiety. Her worst nightmare was finding herself on this remote stretch of land totally under my father's control with no way out. It was on the drive back to Duncan Falls that she mentioned filing for divorce, not so much for support, however sorely needed, as for certainty that he could never concoct a scheme that would make her nightmare a reality.

Mom's attorney was waiting for us as we hurried up the steps of the Muskingum County Courthouse. A little breathless, Mom took the hand he extended in greeting. We followed him across the atrium, into which archways opened, our steps echoing in the building's harsh acoustics. In the center, a broad stairway rose to other levels, and we took it to the second floor. My nerves already on high alert, the strange grandness undermined a hard-earned self-assurance I normally took for granted.

On the next floor, Daddy stood outside a huge set of open double doors. Through the doorway, rows of wooden benches were visible. Images from *Perry Mason* and bars of its theme came to mind, reminding me of the fascination Daddy and I had shared with the main character's legal maneuverings; so long ago it seemed.

Daddy wore a suit straight from the drycleaners and a starched white shirt; possibly one Mom had sweated over at the ironing board. Her attorney's garments and grooming put Daddy's to shame. I'd never seen such perfection—a shirt gleaming white, its collar stiff enough to break, suit and shoes that screamed expensive.

Daddy's attorney, a slouching, mustached fellow in a rumpled suit and scuffed brogans, hurried through the doors. He drew his counterpart aside and the two men conferred for a minute, both nodded, and Daddy's attorney spoke: "We're to meet in the judge's chambers." That took us up another flight in the grand stairway and down a hall. The adults were ushered inside and I was left to a hard narrow bench, obviously designed to discomfit seekers of blind Justice and her scales.

My mind had been anything but quiet since Mom's revelation the day before. No one deserved a reprieve from injustice more than Mom, but no one dreaded spending time on Wolf Creek with Daddy more than I. While I had suffered as part of the wife and child package, as his lone offspring, his blood, I enjoyed impunity from mistreatment. But once his power was absolute, his penchant for cruelty could override any safeguards. Such possibilities plagued me with the persistence of an earwig.

In my earliest years, I had felt connected to the deep voice that read me to sleep many nights and the supporting shoulder that carried the delicious scents of hair tonic and aftershave. On summer evenings we visited the ice cream parlor, and as soon as I was big enough, he taught me to ride a bicycle.

"Does Daddy love me?" I had asked Mom while she trimmed my bangs one evening. I must have been five or so and full of difficult questions. I never had to ask if *she* loved me; she told me so every night as she tucked me in, whether she'd been brought to tears that day or escaped through self-imposed silence. The scissors paused mid-snip. Addicted as she was to the whole truth, never the partial nor the uncertain, she had ramifications to weigh before she could answer.

"I think he does, in his way. It's a selfish kind of love because you belong to him." She cut off her answer at that point, wondering, perhaps, whether a simple "Yes" would have been better. She finished my bangs. I scooted off to bed, feeling less than reassured, too young to sift through all of her words to find the one I sought. Someday I might figure it out, but at fourteen it hadn't happened yet.

The door to the judge's chamber opened, catching me off-guard. I hadn't expected the hearing to be over so soon. Daddy and his attorney stood next to the ornate railing that circled the second floor, smoking. Mom and her attorney approached my bench; Mom's hands were too unsteady to light her Kool, so he came to her aid with a silver monogrammed lighter. Her eyes remained downcast, avoiding mine, but I didn't have time to wonder what was up.

"Francine," the lawyer said, "the judge wants to see you."

Judge Watters, black robes reminiscent of the judge's attire on *Perry Mason*, settled no-nonsense spectacles over keen gray eyes. Standing before the expansive oak desktop was every bit as intimidating as being in an actual courtroom, and the judge's voice seemed to carry the full weight of the law: "Young lady, your father says you can clear up a point on which your parents disagree." Not knowing what response was expected, I remained silent.

Judge Watters cleared his throat. "Your mother is filing for divorce citing two charges. Mental cruelty is impossible to prove. I wish they'd get rid of it. As to nonsupport, she defines this as your father's leaving you and your mother with no means of financial support. In other words, he gave her no money and paid no bills during the time he was away. My question to you is this: Did you ever witness your father giving financial support to your mother during this time? A simple answer will do, yes or no."

Like it was yesterday, I remembered the dark November day Mom and I had gone to Wolf Creek. Daddy had left his wood-cutting and led Mom and me into the kitchen of the old house where he enlivened a banked fire in the coal and wood range with a stir of the poker and the addition of several sticks of wood. Then he reached to the top of the cupboard and took down a pottery jar. From that, he pulled a sizeable roll of currency and began peeling off bills, diminishing the roll considerably, and then handed them to Mom. She examined the money and said, "There's a bill at Huff's Market, too."

"I'll take care of it," he said. "And for God's sake, get this girl a coat that fits." Two more bills joined the others in Mom's hand.

Of course, I thought of Mom's insistence on telling the truth. But had *she* been truthful in *her* testimony? Did she expect me to be? Could I separate this conundrum from my feelings about being isolated with Daddy on Wolf Creek? Before I found answers to the dilemmas flooding my thoughts, I heard my voice responding to Judge Watters' question, "Yes, sir. She did receive support."

I could have added qualifiers, such as "but not enough" or "only that one time." However, that wasn't what the judge had asked. Perry Mason told his clients never to elaborate but to answer the question as addressed to them. I figured that was good advice in the real world too.

Later that afternoon, Mom drove back down Route 60, carrying a burden she had intended to unload that day and yet showing none of the abject misery I'd been certain would follow the outcome. She and Daddy had been in deep conversation just before we left the courthouse, but no way was I getting my hopes up. I'd been sucked down that rabbit hole before. As we crossed the town limits into Duncan Falls, Mom laid a hand on my arm and squeezed. Maybe she did understand, as I was just beginning to, that the heaviest burdens are not imposed by luck or circumstance. We take them on because we think we have to and they become impossible loyalties.

Behavioral Medicine and Oncology, Suite 304

Mariangela dreams of a child
screaming on the porch
of a burning house. She wails with the child
at home alone.

              Here light
gleams through her scans: liver, lung, bowel,
setting pearl suns,   spilled mercury   on black
marble.

           Easter: four
months since diagnosis & the river
rushes backward beneath her: *My*

father was a miner; we
lived in a flimsy company house. Windy
nights he sat up in coal light, afraid
we'd go up in flames.   Father

miner   coal

           light   milk glass.

She dreams

        of the child many times with fear
& once without. *My father*
                who protected us
wouldn't let the house burn.
        In her dreams, he

eats a peach on a boat departing from Italy. What

word is there for a moment of contentment
amid fear?

    Beneath him

the water gleams,   moon ocean, breastbone

    lit up. The side effects

are encyclopedic—Flame skin   heart change

    & withered veins.   Pain-swirled   bowel &

always
the second day writhing. This

is how Mariangela learns

to visualize God

taking the child's hand—*O*

Father   *protect us* *—O Pain*

chest, neck, &

    now brain scans mimic nebulae, sun

glint on fast water   coal fire whitening   to ash.

—Together they walk from the burning.

Strange Bodies

1.
This poem is not about death.
It is about all the days before
or the lifetime that is a single, non-linear day,
whether measured in coffee spoons or ocean tides and howling moons,
my own reticent longing to feel the pull of your neck in my hands
—this dream of a life we share, physical and metaphysical,
in the bodies we could not stop touching,
as if we once believed this is all there is:
sex and skin, soft belly and the angle of legs
that now carry us on foreign bones.

2.
The fact of the matter is
the body operates in total darkness.
All you have been permitted by nature,
or evolutionary biology,
or perhaps by God,
are two slight openings with which to see
everything.
Meanwhile one hundred trillion cells and twenty thousand breaths
circulate inside you every day.

Even when you sleep,
even when you dream you are climbing an ancient tree
in your neighbor's yard to reach for the magnolia blossom,
and your long monkey feet wrap around the trunk,
even as you fall with a flower in your hand and your husband calls
from the kitchen and the smell of toast and coffee
is what you least expect in the cloud forest you fall from,

eighty-six billion nerve cells, and one hundred trillion connections
—more than there are stars in the Milky Way—
scramble at two hundred miles per hour
over a distance of sixty thousand miles,
twice the circumference of planet earth inside you,
to deliver this message in the dark:

wake up.

3
Sometimes you are afraid of what you do not know.
Sometimes you stand on the back patio at night,
look through trees and hear a colorless hum that hides
between whippoorwill and memory,
soon lost in the babble of after-dark arias:
the grand nocturnal opera,
its principal players hiding all around you.
And you, in full view, the dunderhead.
This must be how the spirit feels,
long after its arrival
when the witless body betrays itself
and the two become strangers on a years-long journey
to find each other again.

Ephemera

What I carry has nothing
to do with my purse
but check my pockets.

You may find a penknife,
Chapstick, tissues,
a chartreuse Bic lighter,

small gray stones,
perhaps a few acorns.
Then examine my body,

scars on my face,
1946 forceps, faint
Chihuahua bite on my chin.

Gravel from 1953 in both knees.
Between my shoulder blades,
the tip of a pencil,

impaled in an old
chicken coop, circa 1957,
a 2006 tattoo on my upper left arm.

Now, look closer,
notice I like a lock of hair
on my right forehead,

check my distrust of little dogs,
my distaste for chicken,
my little celebrations of living.

Use your third eye,
see that death has walked
all these miles with me,

taken my earliest loves,
left me to carry
the same loneliness as you.

Donna J. Long

Living and Dying in an Old Neighborhood

Having noticed at most a shadow in the blue
light of the television when passing at night,

you never had a face to match the fading
name on the mailbox. Now you can see

an elderly neighbor has died. At the curb
her collection grows—the story of a life

even living for years on the same street
failed to reveal. Choosing what to keep,

what to discard easy enough: the detritus
of long suffering—crutches, empty bottles

of medicine, the final walker—a history
we wish to leave unrecorded and have

on a designated day hauled away, as if we can
refuse to face the refuse of our own mortality.

This time you wonder at these items left
for trash—a pair of stout boots, a cherry-wood

box with dovetailed joints, a father's workbench
scrawled with penciled measurements. A steel

C still clamped to one side, as if holding years
of grievances a daughter long ago left

to put to rest now turned to grief. A U-Haul
gapes in the driveway. Amid talk of probate

and final affairs, she cautions her own girls
to handle a mother's vanity with better care.

Best Dressed

My mother preferred to go barefoot,
her wide feet permanently stained
by the red clay mud of our hollow—
dirty, and hard and flat as a plank.

Her yellowed toenails were thick as the rooster's spur,
and just as dangerous.
Dad often pointed to the scar on his ankle that
he blamed on her. I imagined her kicking out
when he put his hands on her roughly, or when
he pushed her aside, made her cry.
I wanted to kick him too, and I did;
my small, soft baby feet just made him laugh.

Sometimes, they'd go for a walk, up over the slag heap
and into the hollow beyond.
For these trips my mother wore a pair of old,
black rubber boots, men's,
and a skirt,
and we laughed to see her hobble and lurch
in boots too big and a coat too small.

Only a trip into town or church
could make my mother wear proper shoes,
wide-soled, well-worn sandals from spring to fall,
and clunky loafers, brown and boyish, in the winter.

When I saw the oatmeal sack get low and the coffee tin empty,
I knew my mother would place her shoes by the front door,

the last thing slipped on before going out
and the first thing off
when she got home.

And when the time came,
I chose the blue dress she wore to my brother's wedding,
and my sister chose the shoes.
I didn't say anything to my sister,
just pulled the undertaker aside and whispered
that my mother preferred to go barefoot.

Among the Owls, 1916

Out here we live at the top of a hill with bars on the windows and the forest at our backs. Hell on a Hill, we girls like to call it. Our superintendent, Miss Evelyn, is proud of the fact that they don't have barbed wire strung up here like they do at other places, but the truth is there's no need for a fence to keep us in. There are only two directions in which to run and neither one will probably get you anywhere. One of them is the forest, dark and mean and ringing with screech owls and the scream of bobcats. The other way is the town, which we can see from up here, a cluster of white buildings a ways off with a church steeple knifing up in the middle.

Enough girls have been turned in for the five-dollar reward that we don't dare run into the town anymore. Ever since they started offering that reward the townspeople just dream about a few of us in our uniforms showing up down there so they can turn us in. Girls who have tried to board a passenger train at the station there have some stories.

And bad as the town is, the forest is even worse. Nothing there but briars and ridges with drops liable to break your legs for you, forest so thick you can't see the sun, and rail tunnels drilled through the hills as long and dark as the road to hell. Those rail tunnels are haunted; everyone knows that. Miss Evelyn talks about them often, trying to scare us. She says engineers have got so they recognize the ghosts, and don't even stop if one steps onto the tracks. Says if you hear a train grind to a stop deep in a tunnel, a new engineer unfamiliar with the ghosts is driving the train.

The others, she tells us, have learned to continue, full-steam ahead.

I find this story ridiculous; conductors so familiar with ghosts that they keep running them over, again and again. "What if they're mistaken?" I ask one day at breakfast.

"They aren't, Mabel," says Miss Evelyn, voice a blade. "They know those ghosts by sight by now. And besides, why would anyone alive be in those cold tunnels, stepping out in front of trains? Goodness." And she shudders.

The trains come through here day and night, some of them lumbering freight trains but some full of passengers headed to Cincinnati and St. Louis to the west, New York and Boston to the east. This place is just a long stretch of nothing between those places, blurring past outside the train windows. At night, I lay my head against the cold window in the bunkroom and think of what my brother Anton must be doing. I think of the trains, plowing through all those phantoms without stopping, on their way to the cities.

* * *

My name is Mabel Hilling, and I carve the letters of my first name, real careful, into the wooden beam of my bunk using the redbone pocketknife that I found last fall in the hay barn. The knife is rusted and the blade wobbles but is sharp enough. I hold the blade steady with my fingers, and I carve my brother Anton's name next to mine. I'm not really sure why. It's not like I love him so much or anything, but Anton's the only family I have left.

I've been here for ten months now, and I'll be here until I turn eighteen next year. This place's name is Crossroads School, but it's just a single road that leads up here, and we spend more time hauling hay and hoeing the garden than we do reading books. The sign at the bottom of the hill, outside the gate, reads "Established for the rehabilitation of girls to assist them in becoming useful citizens." We laugh about this, calling each other "useful citizens" even as we try to outdo each other acting the opposite.

I wonder if they're trying to shape Anton into a useful citizen, out there at that boys' home, or just throwing him to work in the fields. I've been thinking about him a lot lately. Anton's always been kind of bad, and after Mother died—well, he got really bad. Turned criminal and started breaking into houses, and I would be the lookout for him. This one house with two stories, I was downstairs while he and his friend pawed through the upstairs bedroom, but I was playing with a hand-crank phonograph downstairs and didn't hear the man come in. I'd never seen anything like one of those phonographs. Couldn't keep my hands off it, trying to make it play something.

Anton was so sore at me for getting us caught that he'd barely look at me in court. He got put in a place about twenty miles to our east, which is like this one but for boys. Word is it's rough there. I've heard people say they have to hose the blood off the walls every day, from all those boys fighting. I don't know whether that's true or not. Once every couple months, there will be a story in the local paper about an escape, or a typhoid outbreak.

Here it's not so rough. Sometimes during dinner a pair of girls will fly across the table at each other, slapping and scratching and knocking over plates, leaving handfuls of hair like tumbleweeds everywhere. No one ever really messes with me though, because I'm in here as a criminal and word is that Anton and I had tried to murder that man. The truth is that Anton had pulled a knife on him, but who knows what he planned to do with it. Said it was self-defense but that don't fly well seeing as we were in the man's house with our pockets bulging with his things. In any case, I play myself up as a criminal, squinting real mean-like at the younger girls who come in. I swear I'm becoming more and more like Anton every day I'm here.

Most of the girls were sent here by their families for some incorrigible behavior, and we call them "indecents." Janice, my bunkmate, won't say why she was brought here, only that her parents had her committed here for "shocking conduct." She smiles when she says this. Sometimes I think she acts all mysterious because she doesn't even know why she's here.

* * *

The cave girls have run away again, and again been dragged back.

Miss Evelyn is fed up with them this time. "You girls act like wild animals," I hear her say to them after dinner the day they come back. "Don't you know how good you have it?" and one of them laughs very loud.

The cave girls are twins, like Anton and me, but identical. Their names are Viola and Mary, but none of us bother to try and tell one from the other. They were sent here for living in a cave with two boys some-where south of here and they're forever trying to escape. Last fall, they ran out into the forest during dinner and were gone for a day. They were brought back after they were spotted foraging for apples on a farm, all scratched up from briars. That time, the newspaper account had referred to them as "two good-looking girls," a detail that kept the pair smug-faced for days. They seem vain about their looks, although I think they look strange, with crooked noses and wide, mushy mouths, as if they had been smashed up against each other in the womb.

This time they'd run into town and tried to board a passenger train at the station, which anyone would agree was foolish. Probably they wanted to get caught. Seems like most of the girls who run away secretly hope to end up in the paper, as if we're all stars in a moving picture and the paper our means of publicity. This time, the paper reported them as "rough girls" who had fought the police, one of them crying that they were "tired of living among the owls." Now we all hoot at them every time we see them. One of them shouts back at us, eyes blazing like she wants to spit in our faces. The other twin is meek and walks with her shoulders curved as if she is trying to turn in on herself.

At night they stay in the cottage locked from the outside, which makes the rest of us think twice about trying to run off. No one wants to sleep in the locked room with the cave girls.

* * *

The sky has been the color of dirty dishwater for months but now it's getting brighter and warmer, patches of green appearing among the straw-colored grass. The creeks rush in the ravines down in the crooks of the hills. The snow has melted, leaving deep sinks of mud that we try to avoid out on the field, or while walking the dirt path from the main house to the schoolroom. Our socks are always soaked inside our boots, the smell of wet sheep's wool lingering in the air.

Janice says there's a boy our age who hangs around by the fence on a neighboring farm, and that he gave her a smoke one afternoon. This is astonishing news, and we make up stories about "cigarette boy" as if he's a movie star, or some legendary creature. We hardly ever see anyone here, and most people we have seen have been hostile. The year before, two girls had pelted some young kids with rocks over the fence of the back pasture. There had been an outcry, with townspeople writing into the school that girls with violent records would be better locked up elsewhere.

"There ain't no boy over in that field," I tell Janice as we fold linens in the laundry one evening.

Janice insists that the cigarette boy does exist, and his name is Quinn. A few days later she tugs on my arm as we walk back to the main house after school. "Quinn's at the fence," she whispers. When I turn I see him, far across the north pastures, leaning on a fence and watching us trail up the hill. From a distance, you would think maybe he was even handsome, although I can tell by the way Janice talks about him that he's not really.

* * *

We're out in the fields a lot in April, and every time Janice sees Quinn she says he tries to talk her into hopping one of the freight trains. He says one of the ones going east can get us as far as Baltimore.

"Probably planning on turning us in," I say.

"Hell, him? He couldn't take us, not skinny as he is. If he tries we'll just punch him and run away. Besides, he can help us hop a train," Janice says. "Knows where all the stations are and everything. Once we get to where we're going we can ditch him."

I think of the town where Anton is, twenty miles to the east. I could hop off, surprise him in the fields as he worked. It seems romantic and daring, like the plot of a moving picture, and I'd never thought of Anton and me as likely stars of one of those. But in the fields, sweating in my smock and shoveling the dark soil, the scenario becomes big and bright in my mind, especially when I hear the trains sighing past behind the hill.

We have new uniforms for spring: White blouses, too big for most of us, with a large neckerchief like the ties worn by scouts, and long cotton skirts. These replace our winter woolen skirts, which were provided by a local sheep farm where we sometimes work. The wool skirts are itchy, like tiny animals with sharp claws trying to climb our legs. We leave them gladly in a big pile in the Great Room.

The newspaper runs a picture of us planting beets in the field, all of us posing in a row, much to Miss Evelyn's delight. We're wearing the same burlap smocks over our uniforms, and our heads are covered with large-brimmed hats that we made from straw during winter. Some girls are turned away from the camera and the faces that you can see are turned toward the sun, so they are mostly whited out as if we have no features at all. I finally locate myself, head turned to the side, looking at the ground.

I wonder if Anton has access to this newspaper at the boys' institution and has seen this picture. I think it's possible, but unlikely. I can't imagine they spend much time reading the newspaper there. I've written to him a few times, on the yellowed lined paper with the greasy pencils they give us to practice our penmanship, but he hasn't written back. I don't really expect him to.

I figure Anton's probably mean enough to get by OK at the boys' school. He used to trap small animals in a cage for fun, and when we were small would pinch me until I bruised. I would always free the trapped animals after he wandered away. But out here, I act like him more and more, pretending ignorance on basic facts of history and grammar, turning in papers riddled with ridiculous errors. Janice and I toss pieces of paper into the rotters' braids. Miss Evelyn tells me that I am becoming coarse and impudent, and I like the sound of that. It sounds like Anton.

Miss Evelyn likes to lecture us over breakfast in the Great Room. She reminds us that girls who act like we do would have been punished severely in the past, locked away in jails and asylums. "But look at us. We're sitting at a table, using real silverware and cloths, and you are receiving an education. You should be glad you are here and not somewhere else." Miss Evelyn folds her napkin on her lap, looking satisfied.

"Well, how do they eat at other places?" I ask, imagining Anton with a row of boys lined up pig-nosed at a trough for meals. "What about the boys' institution? Do they use fine linen there?" Our napkins, not linen and anything but fine, are stained and rough discards from the local sheep farm.

"Decidedly not," said Miss Evelyn, and sensing I am making fun of her, will not comment further.

* * *

Thursday, we slip out the door of the main house after dinner and pick our way down the tree line toward the railroad tracks as it grows dark. A pale moon hangs low in the sky, hollow-looking and imposing, like an eye placed there to watch. Janice says Quinn's going to hop the eastbound freight and he'll help us get on if we meet him down at the freight yard, in between here and the town.

The railyard is on a plot of land crisscrossed with weeds and a barbed wire fence surrounding it. It's easy to hold up and go underneath. There's a little building with a tin roof and a few stray railroad cars scattered around by the tree line. A dilapidated shed stands off to the side. Neither one of us want to admit how spooked we are, standing around in the railyard as the sun sinks behind the hills. The smell of metal and oil is sharp in my nose. I keep thinking I hear footsteps creeping around us, but Quinn is nowhere to be seen. It's getting dark, and the hills and trees around us look so still and dark they could be made of stone.

"Ain't going to show," Janice says. "Train's coming in five minutes."

"Guess we'll just try to hop on ourselves," I say.

"Bull we will," Janice says. "We'd best just go back up there and hope they haven't missed us yet."

"Yeah, end up locked in with the cave girls," I say. "I'm going to hop on."

"Won't," says Janice.

Soon the train comes chattering from the forest to the west. Determined to prove Janice wrong, I go up close to the tracks after the first cars pass by. It's moving slowly, but as it goes by it becomes clear that it would be impossible to climb onto it. Most of the cars are completely closed up, and the ones that aren't look like there's nothing to grab onto, just rattling platforms in midair.

As the last car trails away, a bright light suddenly swoops around from somewhere near the tracks, and I hear a man's voice. "Said they saw them going down this way." Another cries, "There she is right there!" and I see the light of their lantern is focused on Janice, who bolts away down the track and into the trees. I hear frantic footsteps and one of the men cursing. A bright panic coursing through me, I run into the shed and pull the door, squealing on its hinges, closed behind me.

A few minutes later I hear footsteps coming back.

"Damn it," the man's voice says. "I swear I heard that other little girl run thataway."

I realize my mistake in hiding where I did as the cone of light lands on the shed, and fixes there. The footsteps move closer, shining through the gaps in the wood slats. I can hear a man's heavy breathing nearby, hear his boots creak as he crouches down to peer through a gap in the wood. It seems like he's there for a very long time, looking in as I huddle against one wall. I'd pulled my knife out of my boot and I'm ready if they try and come in. "She's in there," he says. The footsteps move and I hear the heavy thud of the wooden door bolt as they force it into place.

One of the men laughs. "Must have been here to meet that boy. Sure is an easy five dollars."

I hear the whoosh of a match as they light their cigarettes.

"Don't worry, little girl," calls the older man. "They'll be here to get you 'fore you know it."

I feel like screaming at them, cursing them until my throat is raw, but I make myself stay silent. The inside of the shed is thick with dirt. The thin moonlight comes through the beams and lights on a row of shovels leaned up against the wall with dirt caked on their blades. There is the smell of very old earth, earth full of bones and fossils that would disintegrate at the touch as if they had been nothing.

They're talking outside about the five-dollar reward. "Newspaper said each," one said.

"At least we got the one."

"Could go after the other one."

"Naw," said the man. "Girl's long gone. Probably headed into town. We'll call up the school about this one. Unless the operator's signed off for the night. Have to wait til morning then I guess."

I hear them spitting hard onto the ground, one after the other. After a while their footsteps recede, scuffing in the dirt. The owls start to question each other again, and I hear a rustle in the leaves that could be a deer picking its way up the hillside.

After a while another train passes so close that it rattles the shed, casting a blinding white light in front of it and blaring its whistle. It's headed to the west, on down through the dark tunnels and to the flatter ground beyond them and then finally to the sprawling city. For a second it slows and I think it's going to stop in the dark, full of all those people in between places. But it keeps up its mindless clatter long after the whistles die down, and then it's gone. I picture its tail end disappearing into the last tunnel, like a thread slipping through the eye of a needle.

I hold the blade of the knife steady and carve my name on the wall beside me. I think of carving Anton's too but I stop myself. Maybe I don't want to see Anton so much anymore, I think, remembering those animals he would trap as a child, how he would laugh at their panic and fear. Here I am just like one of those squirrels or rabbits. I feel like I'll be stuck here forever, if not trapped in the shed then in this place, these woods. I'll be one of those ghosts in the railway tunnel that the trains plow on through. I can see it now as if it's happening. As the train moves through me I'll watch the endless pale faces go by one after the other in the warmly lit cars, all those perfumed and powdered men and women. They will look ahead, straight through me, until the train passes and I stand swallowed by the heavy woods, out here among the owls.

Clefts

As a child I knew
I could disappear
each time the earth
took a breath.

I'd seen cows sucked
beneath their fields,
deer gulped where
the river ran underground.

Where the rifts respired,
I found the gnawed bodies
of tractors, metallic joints
of mammoths, dirt-wet hides
married to the branches
by ice.

Sojourning

An iron trestle spans the gap
between the tracks
on both sides of the river,
a rusted remnant of the coal trains
that crawled the valley walls
beside the tumbling water,
before the veins ran thin
and the mines shut down,
engines cannibalizing coal
and belching smoke on the steep hillsides,
snaking a darkened path on green slopes.
Following my past,
I stand fifty feet above the flow below
on rusted beams of steel,
listening to echoes of rumbling rails
surging up from water rushing rocks
in turn-about eddies.
Suspended in midair,
light-speckled darkness encircles me,
with stars above and fireflies below
to light my way.
Pressing forth,
I long-stride over gaps between the ties,
step and pause, stop and pause,
where only wheels have rolled before,
uncertain of my footing,
yet poised to step beyond. . . .

Coronavirus Melatonin Poem

I'm walking my dog through coronavirus hours,
mostly in the ravine.

He scratches his back on the stone wall going down,
then we bend over the bridge to study the creek,

sometimes hosting ducks, one dull, one bright,
sometimes only us reflected in the water,

though we never tumble, smitten, in.
The creek world, like our own, is upside down,

the sky a nest for trees. After creek, we climb the hills,
weaving through pawpaws, oaks, maples,

spotting a dead campfire in a teepee made of fallen limbs
lifted, leaned, and laced together at the top,

the way that physics joined the earth and water worlds.
The paths keep changing: straight and clear, as if

someone with tidy purpose came before, or curving,
overgrown, veering to the edge of the cliff.

Following the trail to the tracks, we maybe see a train go past.
I wave, and barring the miracle of recognition, am ignored.

I'm writing in a state of melatonin drowsiness,
distilling calm from care, why I'm telling you

on most days we climb down, using roots for stairs.
But days without a train, we walk home on the tracks

because it's bright up there, the path straight. Today
a hawk circled overhead with talons that could lift a cat

and enormous wings, a scary gorgeous angel who would
eat us if we weren't alive or had no place to go.

We are, we have, so we step carefully between the rails,
glancing over our shoulders, treading that wooden way

on sunken ties beat tender by the vagaries of seasons, time,
and the heft of hurtling trains.

View from Quarantine

As if no pandemic rages next door
a child's swing swings as if
she's just jumped from the saddle,

and a grey squirrel scales an oak
unconcerned daffodils are falling
victim to deer, common as a cold

here, where Home Depot's deemed
essential, but I'll not shop for another
reason to repel the living. At 4:30

in the afternoon no one is arriving
home from work. Everyday gestures
now history. Across the ravine
a man hits golf balls into a canvas bag.

They *thunk* like a fastball finds
the mitt, but this is a spring
without baseball. The golfer's son

stands six feet behind his father—less
likely social distancing than staying
clear of the club, or staying clear of

his father's anger if he misses, or
maybe just waiting to be held
in his father's arms as he says,

"Bend your body over your hips,"
or "Keep your chin up," or
"The world is not ending."

The Muse Pedals Up Behind You

Silver bangles ringing at her wrists
like the bell on your first bike.
She stops to pet your pup, says you look
familiar, asks how many snappers
you've spotted laying eggs along the path.
Five, you say. She's seen seven.
You add an eagle; she's seen two.

Once you've told your bike path tales,
you admire her jewelry—bracelets studded
with berry-bright gems; a turquoise pendant,
and beaded earrings so long they brush
her tan shoulders. When she grins
and gives her head a shake to twirl them,
her pewter curls spring to life.

They have stories, you know,
she says in a conspiratorial tone—
*Where you found them, who gave them
to you, who wore them before you.*
You want to show her your rings—
your father's gold pinky with its diamond
that your mother kept until she died.

And the forget-me-not blue oval—
a calm pond set in silver—
your husband gave you
the birthday before his death.
Some say larimar is a healing stone.

And the ring slipped on your finger
years later by your lover—an aquamarine
floating on white-gold waves. Some say
these sea-blue stones washed up from
the spilled treasure chests of Sirens.

You want to tell their stories,
but the Muse is wheeling off,
tires spinning like old movie reels,
like stories with no endings.
Over her shoulder she calls:
Keep counting those turtles!

Running Companion

Every mile run in the rain reveals
another line of a poem. The slant rhyme
of raindrops tap tapping the leaves, the footfall
slap, the splash of the creek running over rocks
brought here in the Pleistocene. I trail rivulets
into the house from my shorts and shirt, grab
my Blackwing and pad while the lines still thrum.

Root Cellar

Descending the stairs, I thought of a morning in August
after milking the last four cows Papaw ever owned.
How we walked in heavy dew, pants as wet as if we'd waded
the creek to the neighbor's farm. A butcher knife dangled
from his hand, and we split a melon straight from the vine,
juice in our mouths slick as warm milk. He told me
graves are cellars, too. Bodies stored on dirt shelves
in hopes of the second coming Mamaw sang about
as she hoed pumpkins and squash, the curved gourds
we used for water dippers. When we buried her,
I placed a jar full of warbler song tucked under an arm,
sweet as sun tea, and another for the winter months,
calls of chickadee a comfort, like hot water poured
over sassafras and stirred with molasses.

It's Summer in 1966, and I Am at Club 250

a bar in Belmont County Ohio, on two weeks' vacation
from babysitting for my mother, a divorced nurse, who
migrated to Columbus in 1959. My grandmother, in her
forties (I am nine) is leaning across the bar, huge pillow
of her breasts pressed against the rail. "Bubbles" they
called her. A farmer's tan connected her freckled
cleavage and neck, my sanctuary lay beneath that great
constellation of bosom.

I can still hear her singing along with Steubenville's
Dean Martin, "Red Roses for a Blue Lady," and smell
the sour stench from the grizzled smiles of her patrons,
tired local truckers and miners who bought me cokes
and candy and sent me to the jukebox with coins.

I remember being scared to dance with them, room barely
lit, corners dark. They were sweet and scruffy as an old
shoe, but alien to me. With Grammie, in her big flowery
muumuus, my head buried in the scent of Coty's Emeraude
Cologne, I could have slow danced forever.

Her day job with Wheeling Stamping was crimping numbers
into tubes of Crest Toothpaste. Every summer she'd share
bar tips she'd saved in coffee cans, so I could go to a Dairy
Queen along National Road in Bridgeport with a neighbor
girl while she worked.

Never once did she mention whether women's wages were less than men's, or why a union worker in a steel industry worked two jobs. Maybe she was lonely.

Her aura enters my dreams at night, calling, her voice full of stars. She shines, humming our song, a cosmic mother. Our harmony of heaven is a scent-filled room with heartbeats teetering at the edge of time.

Strange Fire: The Movie

The Campbell kitchen was jammed with people, equipment, and lights from the documentary production company, Honest Broker Films. The director, Walt Frizzell, the director of photography, Linda Reilly, and the sound director, Charlie Wilson, were accompanied by a small army of crew and onlookers. Caitlin Martin and Roberta Weber, Teresa Bruno-Campbell's friends, stood in the back and whispered to each other.

Standing off to the side was Corny Campbell, the great-great-grand-son of Cornelius C. Campbell, a sergeant in the Continental Army, who built the house in 1814 in a nearly untracked wilderness later called Campbelltown, in Bradford County. Now, deep into his eighties, he leaned against a counter and generally was referred to by everyone in the room as "Gramps." Jared Campbell had fetched his grandfather from the nursing home a day earlier but didn't have the time to return him. Jared never really liked his wife's idea of turning his house into a movie set and fled back to New York City when he received a text that his current big investment deal was cratering.

The production company had brought in a food truck that, along with the other production trailers and semis, clogged Campbelltown Road, all with two wheels digging ruts into the new asphalt and two wheels compacting the grassy shoulder. Teresa, however, had brewed coffee, since it was only 7 A.M., and the group was on the third pot of Gorilla Coffee, straight from New York City. Styrofoam cups littered Teresa's new granite countertops.

Frizzell wore a ball cap with the movie's logo, *STRANGE FIRE*, on it. He wore a rugged Orvis fishing shirt with the sleeves turned up and Orvis cargo pants. His outfit made him look like he'd just come off a few hours of fishing for bass at Black Pond Dam in Towanda. In reality, he lived in Brooklyn, didn't fish, and the only fish he ate was canned tuna.

He frequently checked his Apple Watch which was on the same wrist as a woven leather bracelet.

After consulting with Caitlin and Roberta, Teresa wore her best casual clothes, tight-fitting Gucci jeans and a low-cut, cinch waist blouse with frilly short sleeves. She'd made a point of getting her nails done the day before and had chosen vivid purple lacquer like Jessica Biel wore in a magazine she read. Jared and Teresa's kids, Isabella and Lucas, were standing with their grandpa and alternated between fascination and boredom as the process dragged on since before sunrise.

"Okay people, we only get one chance to do this right, so let's make sure everything is lined up and ready to go before we set the water on fire," said Frizzell.

Neither Reilly nor Wilson moved. They'd both been set for ten minutes while Frizzell fussed around the kitchen.

"Remember, I want authenticity. I'd like the room to look a little less . . . new, just tidy, if that's possible." He surveyed again the gleaming kitchen with its lux appliances, fixtures, and gigantic island with a granite top. "Linda, see if you can do a really tight shot so that we don't see any of the new gadgets or that, that weird faucet thingy." With the drilling company's bonus money and first royalty check, Teresa had redone the kitchen, and ordered all of the fixtures from the Martha Stewart collection. "Also, Charlie, be sure to get the boom in as tight as possible so that we can hear the noise. I suppose we can mix in an explosion sound later but, if possible, I really want authenticity."

Wilson moved the boom in as tight as he dared and looked at Reilly who nodded at him.

"Teresa, hon, stand next to the faucet and pretend you're lighting the water."

Teresa struck a pose near the faucet that made her look a lot more like Vanna White than American Gothic. Reilly ran the camera, then looked at Frizzell, made a face, and shook her head no.

"I don't know, Teresa, hon, this isn't the look we're shooting for. We're looking for gritty, hardscrabble, down on your luck, you know, the typical kind of person who's been screwed by fracking."

"Jared has a new Carhartt jacket in the closet," she said. "Do you want me to put it on?"

He looked at her manicured nails, and perfectly made-up face and hair, then dared a quick glance at her frilly blouse and exposed cleavage. "Yeah, that's not gonna cut it. I'm going for the total look."

"What about me, Mom? I can do it." Lucas was wearing a Star Wars tee shirt, jeans, and sneakers.

"Just stay out of the way, honey, they don't want any kids doing this. They want something more realistic."

"Why wouldn't that be realistic?" Corny asked. "Shoot, we used to do this when I was a kid. I remember one of the Paxton boys, Melvin or Virgil, he nearly set the house on fire, and he might've been six years old . . . younger than Lucas."

"See. I told you," Lucas said puffing up his chest.

Frizzell looked Corny up and down. He was wearing a raggedy work shirt, thermal underwear top, and ancient coveralls. A dirty, threadbare John Deere cap was pulled down over what remained of his thin white hair. He hadn't shaved in three or four days and his face was covered with patches of white stubble. Corny had demanded that he be freed from the nursing home so he could watch the production.

"How about you, Gramps?" Frizzell asked. "I think you've got the right look." He smiled at the old man.

"Done it before, I suppose I could do it again, sonny," Corny said.

"You mean in the past couple of years you set the water on fire?" Frizzell asked.

"Shoot no, when I was a kid, in the 1940s. We had a heck of a time too, until my pa made us stop."

"I didn't know they were fracking back in the '40s," said Reilly. "I thought they were only doing it for like the past ten years when the frackers came to Pennsylvania."

Frizzell leaned in close to her, tapped his forehead and whispered, "He's a little demented, Alzheimer's or something. Nobody set their water on fire until there was fracking. You saw that other movie. I'm pretty sure that was the first time anyone ever did it."

Frizzell smiled at Corny. "Okay Gramps, whatever you say. You can do it. Just be careful and watch out for the pop. Charlie here will have the boom in tight so that we can hear the sound. Also, I'll be off screen and asking you questions about how fracking has ruined everything." He set his coffee cup onto the gleaming new Viking stove.

Corny shuffled over and picked up the box of wooden matches. He looked at the director and said, "You know, sonny, you're only going to have a couple of seconds once I open the faucet. If nothing happens, if there isn't enough gas in the well, you'll have to come back and do it again tomorrow after the gas has built up."

"I know, I know," said Frizzell rolling his eyes. "We've got this, Gramps."

Corny took out a bundle of matches and held them together.

"Wait a minute, what are you doing?" Frizzell asked.

"This is how you do it. It's the only way to be sure you're going to get a big blast."

Frizzell looked at his director of photography and shrugged. Reilly made a face.

"Okay, I suppose that's fine. Charlie, are you ready? If for some reason we don't get much of a sound, mix in a bigger explosion later."

Wilson, wearing oversized headphones and holding the boom, nodded and held up a thumb.

Frizzell looked around the room and said dramatically, "Okay people. Quiet on the set."

One of the interns, a sophomore from NYU, wearing a *STRANGE FIRE* tee shirt cinched at her narrow waist, and Daisy Dukes shorts, came forward and held up the clapper board in front of the camera. "*Strange Fire*, scene twenty-six, take one," she said melodramatically and then snapped down the clapper.

"Action," Frizzell said, then paused and, standing off camera said, "Mr. Campbell, how long have you lived in this house?"

Reilly smiled at her tight shot of Corny's face, grizzled beard and all.

"Well sonny, I'm eighty-six years old and lived here all my life until my grandson and his wife threw me out and made me go live in that awful nursing home. My great-great-grandfather built this house back in 1814. So, Campbells've been in this house for over two centuries."

Frizzell was pressing his hands together, trying to get Corny to speak more quickly and say less. He leaned over to Reilly and said, "We can edit some of this out."

Then, loudly, he said, "And living out here in the country, I'll bet the water was always pristine, really clear, and good, right?"

"I can't honestly say that. It never was great water, truth be told. This is farm land, sonny, not New York City. We've had cows grazing all around our well, pooping all over the place, farmers dumping manure uphill from our well, all that stuff. Frankly, I'm amazed none of us took ill. Folks here must have strong constitutions, that kind of thing."

Frizzell was shaking his head and closing his eyes.

"So, Mr. Campbell, you're going to show us that you can actually light your water on fire. Is that right?"

"Yep, it's quite a sight, sonny. I remember as a boy doing this when I was Lucas's age. My pop told me that he did it when he was a boy, probably back in the 1920s."

"I'm sure whatever you thought you did back then it's gotten much worse since all this fracking came in."

"I can't say. Water was always pretty bad and they were lighting it nearly a hundred years ago."

"All right, all right, Mr. Campbell let's get on with it. I have a feeling we'll be doing a lot of editing." Frizzell paused. "Can you light it on fire for us now. Please?" He paused again. "Remember to look serious."

"Well," Corny said. "Let's see if she'll cooperate."

He took the stack of wooden matches and held them, pausing when Frizzell held up a finger off camera. Then Frizzell pointed at him and he struck the matches. Nothing happened for a moment and then the entire pack burst into flame, like a torch.

"Here we go," Corny said. He held the matches over the sink.

Everyone in the room, Frizzell, the production assistants, Teresa, the children and even Corny leaned in to see the spectacle.

Corny turned on the faucet.

No one breathed.

No water.

Nothing happened.

No explosion.

Nothing.

Corny opened the faucet further. Eventually, a weak stream of water came spilling out of the faucet. Reilly tightened the shot so as not to see the convoluted Martha Stewart faucet, just the water trickling through the aerator. There was no noise in the room, other than the sound of the water hitting the sink and finding its way into the drain. Wilson turned up the recording volume to get the sound of the water gurgling into the drain.

Suddenly, there was a small pop, like a soap bubble popping. Barely perceptible.

Frizzell, who had been holding a rolled-up copy of the script, smacked the papers against the granite counter and said, "Damnit. Not exactly the effect we were looking for."

Reilly pulled out of the tight shot and continued rolling so she captured Corny's face. Unexpectedly, water shot out of the faucet. As the water gurgled maliciously, the tip of the flame, which had pointed to the ceiling, turned sideways and was drawn toward the stream of water. No one had a chance to react.

"Oh boy, hang onto your hats," Corny said, clamping his eyes shut.

Before the camera toppled backward, it caught Corny as his expression changed from a feigned expression of seriousness to a wide boyish grin.

Shooting Rats at the Town Dump with Grandma

Tuesday mornings at the entrance
Jericho greets us in his shack,
lets us pick through other folks' trash
and take what we want.

Three-legged stool
with one leg missing.

Toaster in need
of a rewire.

Old humpback TV
Grandma will frankenstein
with a hanger antenna
so we get reception.

We don't walk downhill
in search of treasure
until we clear the rats.

Rusted-out Chevy Impala
sitting on blocks serves as a blind.
Each of us with a .22, peering
over the sights, fingering
worn triggers.

We hear them chatter
as they slink the rubbish maze.

I shoot first and one flips
like its skittering feet sprung
a trap.

Unlike the rich, with dogs
to fetch ducks and grouse,
Grandma sends me to gather
the dead, to hold them up
by the tails so she can see
the prize.

Limestone Cemetery (Richard's Second Story)

No one was counting on rain.
  Midnight. Tied triple with twine
The blue shoebox—inside,
  Body of a stillborn grew colder,
Heavier—snug under
  A boy's arm. His younger brother led
Them through the woods' uphill
  Paths behind the Presbyterian
White and small and terrible.

Each with a shovel against
  His shoulder searched the family graves
In the clay-poor soil
  When the moon blacked out. And the names.
Heaven kicked and bawled—
  Gruesome work but better than
An early bedtime. They cut
  The nearest plot: whatever happens,
Boys willing to swear
  Sleeping Agnes held her newest
Grandchild in her arms.

Firefly

—*Lampyris noctiluca*

You were my childhood, letting go
of the sun, grabbing at starlight.

I leaned against a window screen
to tally all those glowing bodies.

I knew I counted some two or three times
before I gave in to the spark and shimmer.

When I was young, I believed you
guided souls to Heaven. I believed

June was the only time the gates
of infinite afterlife opened up, permitting

entry to the ghosts of all our loved ones.
My grandfather died in December,

a Sagittarius death. He stayed
six months, a presence among us as we ate

our meals, stoked our fires, slept
unaware of the rest of the world

and its sorrows. I chased you, my arms
outstretched. I held you in my palm,

my fingers curled softly inward
over your luminescence. I put you

in a jar and took you inside.
                        I hoped

you could bring my loved ones home
if I kept you here, in the darkness, beside me.

Sister Blessing

May your clay body remember
it is still supple,
filled with breath.

May the scent of pine
in a snow-covered landscape
awaken new passions.

May the sight of apple trees,
their small blossoms
quiet your mind.

May the chatter of fall crickets
loosen your voice
to offer a new song to evening.

May the flicker of dragonflies
on tall coneflowers
wing new possibilities in you.

May you one day, in early spring,
squat at the edge of a meadow,
recognize in the rising scent,
an ancient memory you can almost name.

Confessions of a Closet Mushroom Hunter

Hunting morel mushrooms is the closest thing to a religion for me. Every April I begin to feel a strange and powerful yearning to crawl through the briar patches of Perry County, Ohio, in search of fungi. If I make it through a spring without suffering the burning sting of briar scratches on my forearms, I feel that I have sinned in some way. In mushroom hunting, pain means success.

The experience of spotting a morel mushroom in the wild existed in my imagination long before it actually came to fruition. In the golden light of my mind, I could see the bulbous, spongy fungus peeking out of leaf-litter beneath a dying elm tree whose bark was sloughing away from its trunk like dead skin. In the clear light of reality, however, I struggled to find a single morel on my own because eons of evolution had endowed this relative of the truffle with an uncanny camouflage that allowed it to elude both four-legged and two-legged predators. Without the sage wisdom of my grandparents who taught me where, when, and how to find these natural Easter eggs of the forest, I may have gone my whole life without ever experiencing the rush of finding a morel for myself.

The greatest single teacher of this catechism of mushroom hunting was my grandfather, Tod Knott. From coal mining to farming, ditch-digging to jerry-rigging, my grandfather did it all. He knew what it was like to live in a world free of nuclear weapons, but he also knew what it was like to live in a world of poverty that eventually led to global conflict and possible nuclear annihilation. Whatever lessons my grandfather learned during his remarkable life were passed on throughout the family with pride, honor, and—most memorably—a bawdy sense of humor that manifested itself in unforgettable witticisms. In my mind, there is no greater example of his teaching ability than mushroom hunting.

Before I contracted morel fever, back when I used to hunt bright orange chanterelles (or "chicken mushrooms" as my grandmother called them due to their resemblance to a cock's comb) that prove to be no challenge at all for a real mushroom hunter, I listened to long conversations between my grandfather and my grandmother about the best places to find morels. They would consult homemade charts that tracked rain amounts for two decades, dates marking when the first mushroom was found in a given year, and the number and weight of each day's bounty. From their conversations, and from reading through their diaries dating back to 1933, I learned that the best time to hunt morels in the spring is when the leaves on the oak trees have grown to the size of a squirrel's ears—when the mayapples, low-growing woodland plants that cover the forest floor like tiny parasols, just begin to open their waxy leaves, after a week of nights when the temperature doesn't drop below forty-five degrees. If any one of these variables is out of place, then no mushrooms. If all these elements are in place and there are still no mushrooms, then of course it's because the wild turkeys beat us to them, or the deer, or the Hinkle brothers, a rival group of mushroom hunters and distant cousins who share a common mushroom hunting gene.

For years, I made countless excuses not to accept the challenge of hunting morels—"It's raining too hard," "I don't have the right kind of hiking boots," "*Land of the Lost* is on"—and refused to go. Slowly, though, my grandfather's words took root and blossomed in some deep, spiritual place within me. One cool, wet spring morning in 1977 when my grandfather, father, and older brother packed themselves in our dilapidated red-and-white 1955 hardtop Jeep and rumbled over the gravel and dirt roads that wind through the woods and hollows surrounding Hemlock, Ohio, I secretly walked to the woods on the other side of the slag heap that loomed across the road from my grandparents' house and began my search. As I stole along deer trails that scarred the ground and wound their way deep into the woods, the branches overhead began to pulse with life, and all the lessons my grandfather had taught me about the flora and fauna he had known since he was a boy worked their way to the surface of my subconscious. In a matter of just a few minutes I spied an entire aviary of birds, including a red-headed woodpecker (or "red-peckered woodheader," as my grandfather called it), a junco, an indigo bunting, and a pileated woodpecker (the bird that was the inspiration for Woody the Woodpecker). Steadily, the trees transformed into more than just generic trees, and I soon found myself surrounded by pawpaws, shagbark hickories, pin oaks, and white sycamores. Even though I didn't find a morel on that first outing, my evolution into a morel mushroom hunter had begun, and my eyes had been opened to a world whose existence I had never before acknowledged.

The first time I found a morel on my own, I found it on one of my secret missions into these woods. I had learned from my grandfather that the most prized tree in the forest for an Ohio morel mushroom hunter is the dying elm tree for the sheer variety of morels that can be found beneath the boney shadows of its withering branches: the gray morel, the smallest and most flavorful of all morels; the black morel, a medium-sized pungent variety; the spike morel, or "pecker head," as my grandfather called it due to its very phallic appearance; and finally the tan morels, the giants of all morels that can, in some cases, grow to nearly a foot in height, and weigh nearly a pound. When I spotted a dying elm that was just beginning to "spit bark" from its highest branches into the sulfurous water of Sunday Creek, I assumed what has since become my standard mushroom hunting posture: down on all fours like a pig rooting for truffles. (Dignity and mushroom hunting are mutually exclusive.) After a few minutes, I saw it just a couple of inches in front of my right hand: a tiny inch-high gray, brain-like fungus in a clump of moss at the base of an exposed root. I stared at it for a moment, blinked a few times to make sure I wasn't seeing a mirage, and then whispered the words of surprise that my grandfather had uttered a thousand times before: "Well up my hairy leg, I thought I felt a mouse!" When I ran back to the house, I didn't tell anyone about my prize; instead, I just added my tiny trophy to the mass of mushrooms already soaking in a pot of cold salt water to coax out any minute insects from deep within a myriad of crevices and folds.

When I finally "came out of the closet" and agreed to go mushroom hunting in the spring of 1981, I brought years of subliminal learning and practical experience to bear. A light rain fell as I, my grandfather, and my older brother—a corporate yuppie who is deathly afraid of bugs but is willing to risk contact with a cobweb for the chance to find a morel—headed out in the Jeep to William's Hill, a wild piece of land so overgrown with briars that just one step into the woods meant receiving a Morse code of pain written across your legs in punctures and scratches.

"I like to hunt in the rain. Mushrooms sprout like wedding dicks in the rain," Grandpa declared. Bawdiness aside, I knew he was right because many of the diary entries for the best mushroom seasons indicated rain. "You always want some rain," Grandpa continued. "But you don't want a toad strangler." I knew, too, that if the ground was too wet, there wouldn't be mushrooms.

We parked the Jeep by a skeletal old barn and hacked our way through the tangle of thorns that seemed to guard the woods. My brother waded across Salt Lick Creek and up William's Hill where a grove of dying elms stood like battle-weary soldiers. Grandpa stuck close to the barn and three or four dead elms near the old cistern. I followed a deer trail to the bottom of the hill and climbed my way back up the other side. In the distance, the chug of an oil well echoed through the woods like a giant metronome, keeping time with one of the dirty limericks my grandfather liked to recite when he hunted: "There was an old woman from Wheeling who had a peculiar feeling . . ." About halfway up the hill I noticed a medium-sized dying elm, a few of its branches bared of bark as if it was wearing a short-sleeve shirt. Assuming my mushroom hunting posture, I crawled up to the tree, my eyes picking between every grass blade and fallen leaf for the small, gray delicacies. Maybe it was because I had never seen a tan morel in the wild, or maybe it was because the two dozen morels that were in front of me were bigger than any morel I had ever seen, but for whatever reason I just didn't believe that what I saw could be real.

"Grandpa! Grandpa!" I yelled. "Found some! Tans! Big! Lots!" I sounded like Lou Costello stuttering as the Mummy, or some thugs, chased him; I couldn't talk in complete sentences.

"You can't shit me!" Grandpa yelled back. "I carry a turd in each pocket!"

I crawled around the tree to look for more. The cold, wet ground made my already sore knees ache, but I didn't care. I was a mushroom hunter!

When Grandpa tramped up behind me, I was still on all fours.

"You're all bass ackwards. You look like the east end of a horse going west," he joked. And when he saw the bouquet of tan giants spread out before us, the words just slipped from his lips the way they had slipped from mine the day I found my first morel: "Well up my hairy leg, I thought I felt a mouse."

We didn't find any more mushrooms that day, but it didn't matter. The mushrooms that we picked at William's Hill weighed nearly three pounds and earned me instant respect as a mushroom hunter, not to mention "a mule's earful" of whiskey from Grandpa and an entry in the family diary. I couldn't have dreamt of a better "first" day of mushroom hunting.

From the time I turned fifteen years old, I've only missed one season of mushroom hunting, official or unofficial. Even though my knees ache a little more, my back becomes a little less flexible, and my eyesight dims just a bit with the passing of each year, the flame of my mushroom hunting desire still burns deep within me. Whenever I see a dying elm tree, I think of morels. Whenever I hear a dirty limerick, I think of my grandfather. And whenever I catch myself droning on to my students about the importance of a thesis statement, I think of the truly important lessons that I've learned while mushroom hunting—lessons about life and family and discovery that have proved more valuable than any academic degree I've ever earned.

Snowmelt Carrion Call

Bloom after uncanny bloom punctuates the crust of old snow
like a pastry chef's stylish swirl, or an unlikely upside-down
exclamation point, always ready to droop over its own opening,

or like a purpling-green bruise to mark the aftermath
of a blow, flesh thick and marred, mottled by its unlikely rise.
Come into my sauna, said the cabbage to the fly:

what other plant can melt the snow, bring the heat of sultry
summer? Where the spathe is scored or damaged, the light
shines cranberry red, neon pink, pulsing to the eye's darkening sight.

Stone flies, blow flies, scavengers, bees—February's fit audience
though few—*Symplocarpus* performs for them, not you:
its spathe a sheath, barely exposing the spadix within,

the spadix that elongated globe, sessile flowers rising from its moon-
white strobe-light surface, like protein spikes on 3D models
of a novel virus, still upstaging our unrooted lives.

Museum Insecta: A Rapture

in response to the threat of the insect apocalypse

It was built in my brain by the age of nine
    and I have filled and tended since then its many exhibits,
countless boxes and drawers of specimens,
    vast displays of butterflies
fluttering to the ceiling
    like a world's sudden exhalation.
I have dusted the glass tops of cases,
    huffing motes off bell jars
under which dioramas of ants and mites
    circus along in dreamtime; I have wandered among
pell-mells of locusts and roaches, crescendos of
    hatching caddisflies—upfloating cloud-glints
of wings, swarms, wonders,
    "grace tangled in a rapture with violence,"[1]
crawling, humming, buzzing, stridulating.

    Swallowtails of silk tissue and camouflage, wondrous;
mantids of photosynthesized metal, wondrous;
    caterpillars of coal dust and emerald, wondrous;
the inhospitable doodle bug, gobbling cousins
    at the bottom of its deadly cone, wondrous;
the paper-pipe tenements of wasps under the
    outhouse roof, wondrous;
thoroughfares of leaf-cutter ants desperate in their
    digestive migrations, wondrous;
the power of beetles almost as large and ripe as grapefruits;
    cadillac beetles, beetles of gin soup and sugar;

1. from *Pilgrim at Tinker Creek* by Annie Dillard

beetles of folded cadmium and beetles of beaten sunlight;
    larvae concocted of licorice and muslin;
skimming jet-skinned hordes of water bugs and whirligigs;
    the wonder of parasites and proboscides;
the elegant extensions of a bee's laden landing gear;
    the sexual attentiveness of antennae;
the aerial adjustments of midges and no-see-ums;

Wondrous the chartreuse enchantments of mulling katydids;
    wondrous the million insect inventions:
grubs, maggots, pupae, hulls of chitin, like antlers,
    like embossings, canister-like eggs
arrayed between leaf-veins like sappers' set explosives;
    the flight, the leap, the crawl,
the squirm, the double-up and loop-out inchworm;
    the subcutaneous, headfirst, dug-in chigger,
the bulging spring chrysalids like tumors of philosophy;

And not the least of which the various disgusts that humans show,
    roach-stomp, fly-swat, ant-poison;
the pummeling car windshield wet after drives
    on the freeway, once smeared with wings, guts, legs—now less
    and less,
the cricket smashed in the basement,
    the wasp freeze-frozen by the house painter,
acres sprayed from planes,
    termites envenomed with dust,
and all the underworld of fear, ignorance
    and the unjust mafia of bad reputations,

and THUS precipitous declines, extirpations, unstoppable
    extinctions,
    the decline of biomass, derangements of whole ecologies,
the rooms of the museum itself growing silent and nearly empty,

world without its innumerable insect histories now,
its irreplaceable pollinators and digesters and buriers,
leaving us behind, starving, alone, in a collapsing world
soon to be dry rock ark of the dead.

Common Pillbug

—Armadillidium vulgaris

Not a bug at all,
     more kin to crab than cricket,
I'm still surprised
     to find you under loose stones,
under planks of wood
     left in the yard too many seasons,
unmoved until today.
     I expected ants or worms. Possibly
centipedes or beetles.
     When I touch you, you flinch,
turn inward, a useless reflex
     against a bird. Years ago,
I rolled your tightly-drawn body
     across my grandfather's driveway,
waited to watch you unfurl
     your body, make
your dizzy way to safety.
     I think I was born to cruelty:
casting out minute bodies,
     focusing sunlight onto ants,
throwing leaf hoppers into spiderwebs.
     My sister said *armadillo.*
My cousin said *roly-poly.*
     My grandmother said *Doodlebug,*
then encircled me with her arms
     as though I would always be safe.

Housefly

—Musca domestica

I learned how to catch this pest
by watching other boys cup their hands,
then swing their arms and clutch at the air.

If they were lucky, there was a buzzing
in their fists, a tickle of life
trapped in their grasp.

But unlike my friends, who pulled wings
from bodies, I walked my captives to the door,
unfurled my hand beneath the sky.

I thought about dragonflies and butterflies,
sparrows and eagles. I thought about angels
torn asunder, unable to stop themselves

from falling to earth. And now,
I wonder if the boys I grew up with
committed this violence to make themselves

feel better about their own wingless bodies.
Now I am trapped in the hand of sorrow,
sure that someone tore away their chance

at flight. I feel their compound eyes upon me,
windowsills littered with hopes,
those clear, forsaken chances to rise.

Nothing Spectacular

Few who have travelled much would call the hills of Greene County, Pennsylvania "spectacular." Even by Appalachian scale they are modest rounded mounds. Their folds conceal no caverns and their streams the humblest of cataracts. Their most rugged features are scattered stony out-crops. Snow never blanches their summits unless it covers the whole scene. While predictably southwest-to-northeast-bearing ridges define much of Pennsylvania's upland topography, Greene County, wedged by West Virginia in the state's southwest corner, is a random morass of hollow and hill. Here, you cannot guide yourself by the lay of the hills. They wander.

Streams here run to the Monongahela River in eastern Greene, and directly to the Ohio in the west. But there's no sharp boundary between those basins, no crest where you know you have crossed a divide. Driving west across the county from the "Mon" on Route 21, you grow accus-tomed to all roadside streams opposing your progress, flowing back toward the way you came. Somewhere past Waynesburg, though, you'll suddenly note that the little creek below the road is tracking your course, sliding west toward the Ohio out of some wrinkle in the hills, trailing you now like a sniffing predator that's snuck up from behind. Where hills wander, streams behave the same, sluggish, "unspectacular" as the knobs they drain.

A widely travelled visitor's first glimpse of Greene County, or much of the Alleghenies' western foothills, might well result in such a mundane impression. But that would be a limiting view, informed by screen shots and televised images of "spectacular" places elsewhere—alpine peaks, tempestuous coasts, lush tropical beach. My way of thinking about land-scapes—of place—holds that "spectacular" is a glib and artificial idea, risen out of casual admiration of famous locations. Through that lens there is no such thing as "spectacular," for to hail one place as "spectacu-lar" risks missing the remarkable elsewhere.

Many places in the American West, for example, are extolled as "spectacular." The West's high mountain vastness, austere deserts, and yawning canyons have been pictured and revered as archetypes of the raw North American continent. Such adulation, though, misses the truth that all landscapes contain, or did contain, their own unique, time-fitted processes, qualities, and elements that make, or made, them function as they must.

The "spectacular" West, as we see it now, is an accident of history, resulting from eastern North America's being "discovered," explored, settled, and subjugated earlier than the West, so that much of what we might have seen as "spectacular" here was gone before we knew to miss it.

Had the continent been settled in reverse, from west to east, and had a conservation ethic evolved before civilization reached the unequalled Appalachian hardwood forest, preserving vast tracts in their natural state in public ownership, we would today celebrate "spectacular" old-growth American chestnut, tulip poplar, and oak stands on Greene County hills in the same way we exalt the Grand Canyon itself. Our experience with woodland here, cut over and regrown multiple times, scourged by invasive plants, does not prepare us to even imagine the forest that cloaked these hills, the forest they are capable of hosting. Were we able, somehow, to visit that native forest, to follow a trail into its depth, we would find ourselves awed, hushed within the native spectacle of this place.

We cannot, of course, walk such a trail. Still, acknowledging what was once here, what could, theoretically, be here again, keeps us open to note and revere the spectacular that remains, and it does remain.

A report of forest resources, produced by the U. S. Forest Service, states that in 1960, 19 percent of Greene County's surface was covered by woodland. Today, reverting woods on abandoned farm and pastureland cover about 60 percent of the county, and it's likely that the 1960 stat already reflected an upswing in forest reversion. The low point in forest cover, perhaps less than 10 percent, probably came around the turn of the 20th century.

Greene County was sheep and beef country then, an expanse of wrinkled pasture, and still was in 1960. Clumps of white sheep ranged over the slopes. Red and black beef cows grazed the bottoms. Dark lines also networked the hills, a grid of big, spreading oaks, beeches, and sugar maples, gigantic even then, left uncut by herders to mark boundaries between their fields. Many of those boundary giants are still there but less conspicuous now, masked among reverting growth that sprang up as hill country sheep farmers died off or gave up.

Walking these woods, searching for morels in spring, or hunting a deer in the fall, you'll know the old trees when you come up under them. Their bulk and reach are so immense that they could be a different species from the saw-timber offspring around them. Their presence will arrest, press you to linger.

A line of gigantic oaks crowns a ridge crest where I have hunted deer over many seasons. The oaks were massive when I first saw them as an excited boy. I know they have grown through the ensuing decades, but any change in their height, girth and spread is imperceptible to me. I see them not so much as individual trees but as the commanding essence of the setting there. They are constants. Sometimes one of the oaks will shed a branch, which falls to ground and dwarfs all surrounding upstarts.

I have often made the climb to the oaks in mid-winter, after all the deer seasons, because it is hard to give up the affinity felt in their nearness. Then, when the foliage is off and your sight-line longer, their size and great age are most striking, the spectacular, masked among the ordinary, made apparent.

Spectacular has nothing to do with scale. Once I sat under those oaks in early fall, when a faint rustle in the fallen leaves was all that kept me from dozing in the warmth of slanting sun. Most woods noises in fall leaves betray rapid bursts of movement—a chipmunk's darting, a squirrel's leap and scurry. This was different, a barely perceptible inching, a hushed lurch, announced by some single dried leaf coiling against another, so faint I could have mistaken it for an aberrant circulatory rumble inside my own ear. Yet, that determined rustling grew nearer, mere feet away.

Finally, I saw a leaf move, barely, and a dark mound, fist-size, lurched into view at my outstretched feet. Then, a shining eye, set in a docile head, rose to survey the ground, and a yellow-mottled shell settled itself for the next step. A box turtle, making its slow way forward, the soft rustling's stolid author.

I reached out and picked it up. It felt heavy for its size, as box turtles do. This was one of the rare box turtles that do not withdraw inside their sealable shell when handled. Its red eye glared from its beaked and scaled head, its bright orange legs flailed a deliberate turtle-flail, and clawed toes scratched across my skin.

The domed carapace was handsome with yellow, rune-like markings on a brownish-green background, each rune pattern enclosed in a geometrically distinct scute, and each of those ridged by faint concentric growth rings. I turned the turtle over to examine the plastron—its underside—and the head strained to right itself, to continue its reptilian glare.

My fingertips played across the plastron's dark surface, which seemed to absorb light within itself, outwardly translucent over an opaque and featureless black. Once I'd stroked the plastron, I could not stop doing so for the sheer tactile mystery of it. It was the smoothest surface I have ever felt, so smooth there seemed no palpable boundary to it. With fingers resting on it, I could have believed I had not yet touched it. There was no sensory report of contact, only a disorienting sense of something outside my experience, beyond its possibilities. My fingertips caressed a surface polished against the cellulose of a million leaves, dragged across the buffing of algae and moss, for days and nights within these woods. In its startling smoothness, a box turtle's underbelly is as spectacular as the Grand Tetons' jagged silhouette.

Spectacular can be as much about ecological context as it can be held in the hand. Often, I've sat among those big trees and admired fox squirrels, a creature that appears entirely different in different regions. Geneticists believe fox squirrels are still trying to work out their evolutionary response to the changed eastern forests that followed the last ice age. One species everywhere, fox squirrels are black across much of the South, and silvery-gray along the Atlantic coast. In Appalachia, fox squirrels are a warm rusty-orange, blending to sulfur yellow on the belly.

Their tail here is orange, with a ragged black border. Think "fall foliage" in fur; that's an Appalachian fox squirrel.

Fox squirrels everywhere, no matter their color, are also big—the biggest tree squirrels in North America. They can weigh nearly twice as much as the more familiar gray squirrel. They're also more sedate in behavior than gray squirrels; they seem to never hurry. They'll sit motionless in one spot, evidently entranced, for long stints.

When I hear an unhurried scratching on bark high in the oaks, I know a fox squirrel is near, maybe descending to forage on the ground. The ensuing moments will often reveal to me, brought up a squirrel hunter on the Greene County hills, the spectacular in the form of arboreal rodent—one whose presence tells a story of context, process, and time. If the squirrel hunches downward toward me, then pauses, legs and tail outstretched against a sunlit limb, head up and alert in the sun, as if it were reveling in the pleasure of autumn rays, which it well might be, I am myself entranced in a spectacular presence.

Fox squirrels are less abundant here than when my grandfather took me to hunt squirrels under those oaks. But that's less tragedy than it is simple consequence. Fox squirrels prefer a different kind of woodland than grays do. While gray squirrels favor extensive forest, fox squirrels thrive best in scattered woodlots and along woodland edges—the kind of habitats that dominated the hills when sheep- and cattle-grazing were at their peak, and in their early decline.

I have read, and this excites me as one of the most spectacular concepts I've encountered about this region, that before European settlement, fox squirrels lived along the ever-shifting eco-border between wet eastern forest and dry western prairie. During wet cycles, forest probed west toward the Mississippi and beyond. In dry times, forest retreated eastward, back toward the mountains, and grassland claimed the vacated ground. For thousands of years along that capricious border, a blurred mix of woodland and grass was trod and grazed by bison. Fox squirrels thrived there, their numbers following the big oaks and hickories eastward or westward along the wavering grassland-woodland interface. There's a sense of spectacular in knowing that the patchy jumble of woodlot and pasture that cloaked Greene County's hills, where I shot fox squirrels as a boy for the family pot, where Angus and white-faced Herefords grazed in their placid mimic of bison, was a vestige of that prehistoric landscape. That feels no less spectacular than the migrations of whales.

The widespread reversion of abandoned rangeland to forest since 1960 favored gray squirrel expansion while it reduced habitat for fox squirrels. Since that's a natural consequence of forest reclamation, the fox squirrel's decline is less of a sting. But another factor in the decline, the explosion of invasive plants here within my lifetime, is dreadful. Fox squirrels prefer an open understory—park-like is one way their ideal woods are described—where they can forage on the ground and watch for predators. Today, any place within these young, reverting woods where sunlight can reach the soil is invaded by multi-flora rose, barberry, and garlic mustard—thorned, snarling, or astoundingly prolific exotic plants that got a foothold within the last 40 years and now can't be stopped. Their tangled thickets clot the hills under the trees, too dense for fox squirrels. To call this phenomenon "dreadful" is, of course, a human judgement, and far from the catholic lens advanced here. Considered in that light, the rapid adaptation to and dominance of Appalachian woodlands by invasives like multi-flora rose and garlic mustard is, itself, a biological achievement of spectacular scale. Still, I yearn for the more native woods I knew in my youth, whose plants were less rank, distributed over the land not by a penchant for utter dominion, but by some unseen protocol of shared space and light, known only among their various kinds.

That yearning demonstrates what a great debt we owe those prescient conservationists of the late 19th century who worked to preserve Grand Canyon, Yellowstone, the Great Smokies, and so many other landscapes where native process still reigns, where it can be acknowledged and understood for the rightness it represents. We need those places in our increasingly artificial world, for all manner of reasons. Despite my questioning here of their "spectacular" reputations, my direction of attention elsewhere, I do not wish to diminish their importance. Their importance is beyond words' ability to dim. But those preserved landscape fragments cannot accommodate all of us, and I've never found satisfaction in the idea that we benefit from wild conserved places "just by knowing they are there." I need contact. I seek immersion. Since I cannot travel to icons of landscape or of ecology every day, and because those hallowed places can't serve all our needs for contact, for immersion, without sacrificing themselves, there is also importance in cultivating an eye for the spectacular that carries on all around us. I first sensed that universal "spectacular" in the, some would say, unremarkable hills of Greene County. That was, I am sure, an accident of circumstance. Places much like Greene County, Pennsylvania rim the Appalachian margins. All hold the spectacular within themselves, different from Denali or Yosemite only in scale. Up close, spectacular is wherever you find it, wherever it finds you.

Lake Paradox

This is how you will go.
From Dark Harbor you will ease
out onto the sunlit lake.
As you row, you may feel the currents
of the Schroon River pulling you
in another direction. Resist them.
They have their purpose, you have another.
Row across the waters to the Narrows
until you find the trail to Peaked Hill.

There you will go by land,
hand over hand, foot over foot,
until you make a ladder of the earth.
From the top you will command a view,
wide yet obscured by the years and the trees,
for they have grown, too.

But then you will descend from the sky,
down the ladder of earth until you return
to water. Push out again. The winds,
which you did not notice gently
upon your cheek as they carried
you here, will now blow
against you rowing backwards.

Then begins the trial, to find a way
across dark waters to a place
you did not know and cannot see.

River Speak

He said to bathe with birds
along the edge of light. Run with dogs,
he said, to open your lungs and eyes.
He said my name lies under a stone in
a cemetery yard. Forget about questing
for words. He said that girl to my right
will birth me before a fire when our
breath is most hard. He said to give up
walking on water, shooting a buck,
climbing a ladder to the stars.
He said all food flows like a spring,
think on nothing while you swallow.
He said all balls are meant for play, all
song for release. He said wipe my shoes
before climbing into bed with your dreams.
Take your time, he said. The weather
teaches all that you need.

Midsentence

Water talks slowly, murmurs
its way down the chest
of the mountain, for centuries
licking holes through stone,
beginning to shape the word
bridge, which a fox trots across
only after half the moon
breaks away.

Out the Window

She wanted to fly—
a monarch, a raven, a red-winged
blackbird, a goldfinch
or at least an angel.

Birds appealed to her more
than angels.
She had held them in her hands
when she lifted them
off the porch, their eyes dull,
their bodies limp and still warm.
The cruel window
invisible until too late.
Each bird seduced by something
not seen.

She carried them
one by one
to the marsh
and laid them
gently
among the pirate daffodils,
among the insistent forget-me-nots.

She wanted to fly—but
instead she learned
first to hide, to secure
a corner in a cornfield
when the tassels were golden

and the field was hard
with August heat and old sun's
insistence.   Or she'd climb three
flights of stairs to the belfry,
her Marlboro pack in her one hand
and her 6-ounce coke in the other.
She learned to be silent
in hallways and classrooms,
on the hockey field
on the basketball court
in the presence of others.

She learned to be quiet when
she played Beethoven, as if
even her fingers making noise
by hitting piano keys
was really silence from her.

She wanted to fly, but she could not,
except at night in dreams laced with downdrafts.

Instead she became a runner.

She ran away from cousins,
and sisters, and would-be brothers.
She ran away from chickens and the rooster,
from strangers and spotted
leopards who lived in her heart
after she had seen their pictures
in magazines.
She ran out of classrooms and
down sidewalks away away
away from herself and her
banging swollen heart.

She did not ask permission
from anyone, and she accepted
whatever punishment was doled
out.   How could
she speak in Algebra II and announce that she
was suffocating, that there was no air
and everything was so loud
she couldn't think?

She could walk out of the classroom—before
she took off. Her feet almost as good
as wings.   Detention,
nurse's office, conversations with
the dean—as if she would tell him
anything, with his licorice candy
and ferret face—nothing stopped her.

At college, the last time she ran
out of a room, she really had no choice.
She could see the walls around her
disintegrating so she took the fire
escape.   She found her
car and drove and drove and drove.

She went to anywhere without a past,
somewhere without people she loved,
and she began to breathe again
until she grew lighter and lighter
and wings began to sprout—
people thought she had gotten
too thin, that her shoulder blades
protruded, but they were wrong.

She was preparing to lift off.

Her eyes turned from blue to gray to silver.
Her skin became the texture of feathers
and she blended into the November sky.

Credo

Look at your own ponds, whatever shape they take.
—Lauren Groff, on Thoreau

Granted that my yard
is a multiverse of its own,
bird, worm, grub, beetle,
mole, mouse, groundhog,
sycamore and hemlock,
fungi and nematode,
immortal herds of tardigrades—
granted this, I cannot exhaust in my lifetime
what all there is to see and say.

Granted that the cold cathedral
of my basement, its foot-square
white oak pillars, its vaultings of rafters and
joists, its serpentines of pipe and wire,
its alcoves of camel crickets
and the saints of dust—
granted this, I will not discover it all
in my lifetime; it is
a cell of infinities,
museum of itself.

Given that
my days and works,
whatever shape they take,
add up to nothing
and yet everything—
what I write, what I hoard,

what I cast off
into the landfills and dumps
and suffering rivers,
what I misuse and overuse
or fail to use,
pens, machines,
forests, shale plays,
solar panels,
old lumber,
cans of hardened paint—
granted all this,
I remain unfinished,
the draft of a draft.

I move and stay put,
scribble and sing, love and eat,
until I don't.

So if I manage to return
as a morning lush with dew
and birdsong,
let there be a pond nearby,
where some young one, listening,
may bathe and be blessed.

An Interview with Patrick Farabaugh, Author of *Disastrous Floods and the Demise of Steel in Johnstown*, The History Press, 2021

The obvious question: what sparked the interest to write *Disastrous Floods?*

I was born and raised in the Johnstown area, and I heard many stories about the 1977 flood and the steel and coal industry in the region while growing up. My grandfather, John Earl Boland, was a coal miner in the area for four decades and I had heard lots of stories from him about the industry. I had also heard stories from my other uncles who worked in the mills and the mines.

After reading David McCullough's *The Johnstown Flood* which meticulously chronicled the Great Flood of 1889 and the iron industry in the region during the late nineteenth century, I decided to take on this project. While I do write about the 1889 flood in the first chapter, this book sort of picks up where McCullough left off, sharing more on the subsequent floods and the steel and coal industry in Cambria County.

This is also a history of great social divisiveness, something we can see parallels to today in Johnstown and nationally. What can we learn?

There are always lessons to be learned from history, and Johnstown's story is no exception. When a community—or a nation—experiences polarized politics and economic hardships, disagreement and discord typically follow. That's what happened in Johnstown throughout much of the U.S. labor movement.

At the beginning of the movement, Johnstown-area business and clergy members overwhelmingly supported management in the battle initiated by labor leaders to improve working conditions and quality of life for mill workers and miners. The prevailing sentiment of these two groups was that if laborers wanted more money, they should stop complaining and do a better job of saving it. This attitude within Johnstown's white-collar community sewed seeds of discontent in the city's working-class sections. As the pendulum swung decisively in labor's favor over the course of the movement, attitudes of both white and blue-collar workers in the city shifted. A deeper appreciation emerged among folks in the region that no side was fully right or wrong.

Vignettes in the book add to some of the vivid detail, particularly those folks who lived through the disasters to extreme old age. They still identified closely with the town, despite the catastrophes. Is it fair to say they exemplify something about determination and the community?

Without question. They are representative of an incredible determination that is seemingly part of the DNA of the people of this region. Almost to a person, people born and raised in the Johnstown area have a resiliency and fortitude about them.

Like Daise Heslop and Frank Shomo, my grandfather embodied this determination. In the fall of 1962, Pappy was working at Bethlehem Mine No. 32 beneath the village of Revloc. He suffered a cervical fracture when a rock fell on him from the ceiling of the mine. He was carted to the surface and taken to Conemaugh Hospital in Johnstown, where doctors drilled holes into each side of his head and placed him in traction for six weeks.

Pappy had to relearn how to use his hands and fingers and one of his feet was temporarily paralyzed. Like many other miners and mill workers who suffered serious injuries on the job during this period, he needed to design and implement his own physical therapy regimen. He re-learned how to use his hands by hitting a punching bag; he strengthened his upper body with a weighted pulley system; he worked to regain the use of his fingers by squeezing tennis balls. He created an electrical stimulation device to help generate nerve growth by shocking himself. Pappy eventually regained the use of his fingers and he returned to work six months after his accident. This is the type of determination that people from the Johnstown region have demonstrated again and again and again.

You identify a number of failures on different levels: labor, management, technology, economics, and even bad luck. What are some lessons that can be learned from what seems now to be an obvious combination for disaster?

Well, as you note, I believe it only becomes "obvious" in retrospect, so avoiding hindsight bias is really important.

This is a critically important question as our nation and the world continue to move toward greener energy sources. I think the most important takeaway from what happened in Johnstown and other Rustbelt cities is the value of humility among business and political leaders. If our leaders appreciate that no one has a monopoly on the one right answer or right approach or can't-miss solution, I think this would be an incredibly valuable lesson.

Northern Appalachia has significant overlap with the Rust Belt more generally. Can you comment on the experiences of communities in Northern Appalachia during de-industrialization?

It has been—and continues to be—a steep climb out of a deep hole for most Rust Belt communities across Northern Appalachia and beyond during the last half century or so of de-industrialization. When a community hitches its economic wagon to one industry and fails to diversify, once the economic driver that carried that community declines, there are consequences, often dire ones.

This is magnified when leaders fail to identify the warning signs within a particular industry. And when I say leaders, I am referring to both industry and political leaders. And one of the big things that I think many people don't realize is how long it takes to recover. When people move away from an area because jobs dried up, that population doesn't recover overnight. When downtowns decay and homes are abandoned or foreclosed on, it's not like you can wave a magic wand over the region so new jobs and opportunities emerge. People need to move back or settle into the region. Blight needs to be cleaned up. A tax base needs to be reestablished. This takes time. Recovery takes generations.

November

It is November
and the child's socks are falling down.

On Cranbrook Circle,
houses appear quiet outside.

Inside,
the girl's mother plays *Moonlight Sonata*.

Her metronome spine
a kind of solace

against the chaos of murder
in Dallas.

Television images of people crying—
like her mother crying,

following notes on a page,
knowing exactly

what sound comes next
and when—

slip into the house, subtle as memory:
a continuum of black and white.

The line between
sanctuary and danger

at once impalpable.
Is life this uncertain?

Golden Triangle

Where the Allegheny and Monongahela Rivers join and become the
Ohio River

Pittsburgh 1968, new academic year.
Driving back to campus we're steeped
in an umbra of smog from J&L Steel.
Black columns of smoking stacks soar,
tapered, elegant, soot like thick fur.
Reflected off the river heartbeat flames
of the blast furnace pulse a molten blend
of desire and ignorance.

My boyfriend and I are parked
in the campus lot. He's my first boyfriend,
I'm his first girlfriend. Nobody else around,
and after a session of heavy petting
I'm thinking I need to get back to the dorm
before curfew. Suddenly he starts telling me
what happened during our summer apart,
how he was in the home of a local girl,
in the kitchen talking with the girl's mother,
how he liked talking with the mother.
Then the girl called down for him
to go up to her bedroom.

Leaving the kitchen and climbing
the stairs, he hears the girl's voice:
I'm here, in my bedroom, come in.
He stands in the doorway
and stares as she strips down
to her bra and panties.

As he speaks to me, his tone
is somber. He looks at the
car dashboard, not at me,
but I can see his face is sad.
His shoulders hunch over,
and that makes him seem older,
burdened.

Why are you telling me this?
He doesn't answer. He has reasons
but won't or can't say them:
He wants me to undress for him,
do whatever else she might have done,
which means for me not to be me
but to be her—her instead of me.
Or, he wishes she and I could merge,
flow together like rivers and become
a new composite girlfriend.

We broke up, slowly over the next few months,
long talks that stayed on the surface like slag.
What if we'd understood? If we'd been able
to dive into the truth? Would it have made
a difference? *What if's* pile into logjams.
Decades later you try but you
still can't unclog things.

End of that year I transferred to a college
back East, met someone on the rebound,
stayed a virgin straight through
to my disaster of a wedding night.
Four years later, divorce.

I don't know what else happened
between my boyfriend and that girl,
or if he ever saw her again.
From what I heard, he stayed in Pittsburgh,

went on to law school, served with honor
as a Marine in Vietnam, married,
had two kids. He died recently.

By mid-1980s the mills were shut down
thousands lost jobs, workers and families
went on welfare, many forced to move.
I've seen photos of the abandoned J&L.
It's like seeing the lonely carcass of a
magnificent beast brought down by poachers,
remains scavenged, valuable parts pilfered.

A Visit to Modern Pittsburgh

Life is very different now, isn't it,
here at the confluence of the great rivers?
In winter we bask in softly blown heat,
and summer allows us to walk unbrambled to The Point,
or idle inside, safe from the sun's burning power,
where we quaff shining drinks, sweet or potent.

Each time I travel to the Commonwealth of William Penn,
the State of Brotherly Love, I wonder about the first people—
Monongahela, Susquehanna, Allegheny.
I wonder if they know what happened to their land,
if they see these giant pre-wreckages of glass and steel
obstructing the flowers and the trees all around the rivers.

I wonder if their tears are not sometimes
accompanied with wry smiles
at how the white conquerors
have punished themselves and their descendants.
For would it not be somehow better to sweat our summers
and swat loathsome insects,

endure bitter winters that freeze the mud
in the walls of our wooden houses,
so that we might hear the rolling rivers sing at night
to the bright moon, who showed us a beauty
we have not regained?
Was it not good to live with our brother the oak

and our sister the beech all around us as good friends?
Was it not in some ways better when our food

came fresh from clean rivers, towering forests,
and the unpolluted soil?
Was it not in some ways better when our shaman and our chief
made their beds in the nearby houses, and we all ate from the

same pot, and sat close around the same council fire
to decide what to do?
And do the old ones not still hold their councils
at night on the distant hills,
or even here in the concrete city,
wherever two or more trees are gathered together?

Gabriel Welsch

Why the State Has *Sylvania* in Its Name

We occupy the edges,
the mountained remove.
The news twitters in, or not.
Even the turnpike makes no
direct passage. The breeze
decrees, decrees, decrees.

Adept at stasis, we age
among the valley's trees.
Each barn breathes remnants
of the century of steel: rusted basket
of a tractor seat, combine teeth
gouging the brambles, chewing
the drift of plastic bags and bottles.
Gabby as acorns, we don't hear
our stories. The leaves rustle them.

Wherever the town has wept,
sucker stems crowd the sidewalk.
Let's marvel at the taste of such a place:
the algal fur of old shingles,
car door rind, suet of a tilting
woodpile's mushroom scrim.

Wherever fire raged,
the birches flare as ash.
Wherever trunks fell for masts,
the redbud weaves its way.
Where the oaks fell for fire,

furnaces stand, each impotent
crypt a chapel of charred stones.

In the resurrection of this place,
no shade is older than 100 years.

The Losing Tree

I grieve the last Elm
that grew here, hiding from the bark
beetle blight that took her sisters.

It grew in that sinuous lover's grace,
her limbs entwined with her limbs—
a pose that made me hug myself.

Whenever I gazed at her, I longed
to be like her, her trunk
branching into two

with one resting onto the cradle
of the other, a torso at leisure
between two upthrust thighs

the three reaching not
for the sky but for the whole
of the wilder world it was

a part of. Now those leaves
and their snuggled limbs,
lie across the lawn.

When the grass grows through
I'll haul out the saw.
Until then, I sit shiva

in the company
of the long-trunked locust—
ragged and winter weary—

that has stood by her
all these years. I wonder if he
or I will be next to go.

Valerie Bacharach

Almost New Year's Eve

Damp and cold in Pittsburgh, another grey sky.
At the bird feeder: a female cardinal with her garish orange beak,
a house wren, and two starlings who seem to snarl
at the other birds, staking claim to seeds.
Moss the color of Ireland grows on stones.

I'm printing recipes for New Year's Eve, the only revelers
my husband and me.
Olive tapenade, endive with orange and walnuts,
a new cocktail, Boulevardier, and I remember

a New Year's Eve in Paris, walking narrow streets
with my husband, every tree strung with white lights,
the sounds of laughter and music escaping into air.

Once we stood on a balcony in Porto, watched
fireworks over the river. Drank wine
from the Douro Valley, ate local sardines and olives.

I sit at my desk, surrounded by photos of my beloved dead, burn
an incense stick that scents the air with piñon.

A bird flew into the window earlier, one of the mourning doves
that skims the juniper, eats seeds from my neighbor's steps.
A few small feathers still cling to glass, sway back and forth

in wind, as if still attached to wing, as if able to fly.
If I collect enough I could weave them into shawl, wrap
myself in flight.

Sharing the News

When Denise, who cleans for me,
said Obama was a "Muslim
bent on our nation's destruction,"
I could have argued, hauled out
my arsenal of academic rhetoric,
not to mention a few *true facts*.
Instead I suggested we agree
to disagree, which I admit
is the ultimate dismissal.

Yet there is much we share.
One year our husbands both had cancer.
Hers got sick first, but mine was first to die.
That winter, before she started the vacuum,
we'd warm hands around coffee mugs
talk of what we'd lost, and watch
the cardinal couple nipping seeds
from the feeder her husband
built when he had to quit working.

She's Fox News all the way; I'm PBS.
But the news that means most to us today
is about the bald eagle she spotted standing
in a stubbled cornfield on her drive over;
my startling a doe nibbling barbed holly
leaves beside the porch this morning;
and the great horned owl, and then her mate,
dropping like heavy angels into the dark
morning arms of my white pine.

She knows more than anyone
about the birds—who mates for life,
who migrates, who eats other birds' eggs.
So how could she, who thrills to tell
of mom and baby wood ducks floating
on her marsh, sell her gas rights to frackers—
some of the worst predators on the planet?
I ran them off in a hurry when
they sniffed around my acres.

My pension pays Denise's wages
and the mortgage on my house
that's probably too large for one person.
I know I should feel guilty, but I love
these rooms, whose surfaces she shines
with her dust cloth, too much to trade
for a smaller carbon footprint
and a cleaner conscience.

When her husband died, Denise sold
his truck and guns to pay off
medical bills, saying he deserved
to die with dignity. The money she got
for gas rights, she tells me today over lunch,
allowed her to stay in the small house
they'd long ago rescued from decay.
We eat salads outside by the goldfish pond,
watching as they glint in sunlight,
vanish in shadow—our silence
a page of shared wonder.

Beyond Duality

I turned into the long driveway of the house not visible from the country road. I parked in front, retrieved my small harp from the back seat, donned my mask, and walked to the door. I could hear the beat of my heart in my chest; the rhythm pounded in my ears as I approached the door and rang the bell.

The man yelled from inside, telling me to come in. I entered and walked straight down the dim hallway into a room where the patient lay in a hospital bed. She wore the same red, white, and blue patriotic t-shirt she had on the last time I visited. I sat down facing her, pulled my little harp out of its case, and began to play. The patient looked at me with beautiful brown eyes, and my heart melted. The heaviness and constriction of fear dissipated in the wake of her gaze. I began to play and sing. She maintained eye contact, sometimes watching my hands, and occasionally smiling and laughing. I could hear her husband banging pots and pans, making noise in other rooms. I held this in my awareness while I played, but I maintained my attention on the patient.

* * *

It is less than a week after the school shooting in Uvalde, Texas, where nineteen children and two adults were gunned down in a classroom of Robb Elementary School on May 24, 2022.

I am visiting hospice patients in rural northern Cambria County in southwestern Pennsylvania.

The brilliant blue sky and puffy clouds provide a backdrop for the rolling hills, barns, and farmhouses quaintly tucked back from the road as I drive through this area.

The vast expanse of sky and the tidy farmhouses and farmland look like something from a postcard, except for the Trump signs. Faded signs remain from the 2020 election and still are largely and prominently displayed in these rural areas. Flags with the image of an assault rifle and

Trump's name are present, and there are a couple thanking Joe Biden, with his head in a turban, for "Making the Taliban Great Again," as well the confusing phrase, "Let's Go Brandon."

In my tiny blue dot in the valley of Johnstown, Pa., surrounded by the Appalachian rolling hills and a sea of red, the dissonance and the polarization have gradually become more pronounced in the last several years. The intensity finds more momentum with the massacre of folks of color in a supermarket in a predominantly black neighborhood in Buffalo, New York.

Accustomed to these scenes of signs and flags as I am, today each sighting adds a heaviness to my body. My heart constricts, my breath is shallow, and there is a sick feeling in my gut. There have been, in the week following Uvalde, shootings in Philadelphia, Michigan, Alabama, Tennessee, California, Florida, Illinois, Colorado and, most recently, in Oklahoma at a hospital. Sorrow, rage, and despair reside in my body, heavy and tight. The day here looms before me. I concentrate on driving, breathing, and resisting the urge to turn on the car radio to listen to the unfolding details of the latest tragedies.

As I drive, I can picture the last house I am to visit—a house tucked way back from the main road. A home where there is disarray with a man trying to care for his wife who is bed bound with Alzheimer's and requires care 24/7. There are dirty dishes everywhere. Laundry is strewn throughout the house in piles. The outside, however, is neat and well-tended with a work shed, firewood pile, and tractor beside the house. There are no flowers, but a vegetable garden on the side of the split-level home.

My mind's eye recalls rifles stacked in a corner of the upstairs living room—not locked in a case but propped in a corner. During my first and only experience in this home several weeks ago, the man was clearly distraught and challenged by the situation. Our staff had spoken of this and were working to find more support, but he stubbornly insisted that he had everything under control.

The story my mind keeps telling me about loaded guns in homes with volatile men that live in communities with Trump flags has me on high alert. I focus on slowing my breath down and seeing the patient.

* * *

I finished playing my harp. I played longer than usual, partly because the patient responded positively to the music, and partly because I dreaded walking through the room where the guns are propped in the corner. I put my harp back in its case and wished my patient peace and blessings. I stroked her brow while her brown eyes looked deep into mine. I walked down the hall. Her husband met me in the room with the guns stacked in the corner.

Only there were no guns.

There were walking sticks.

Long sticks used for support for hiking on trails with uneven footing. I carry one in my car and have a couple stacked in a corner in my own home.

In addition, the room contained a Native American flute, a guitar, issues of Mother Earth News Magazines, piles of books on homeopathy, plant and herbal medicine, objects that are familiar and present in my own home. These objects slowly landed in my visual field, and the dread slowly seeped away.

I breathed fuller and deeper. I felt my feet on the floor.

I looked at my patient's husband. He wanted to talk about healing with music, plant medicine, and more. I listened as my nervous system settled, the heaviness and constriction releasing in the room with walking sticks in the corner next to a guitar. Eventually, I walked down the steps and out the front door. He followed me and stood watching at the doorstep as I drove away.

I drove away, past Trump signs, past rolling hills under blue skies.

I drove away dissolving the fixed certainty of my mind that convinced me that what I saw in the corner of a home in rural Pennsylvania fit neatly and squarely with assumptions I make every day about people.

I drove away with curiosity, humility, and a spaciousness for what lies beyond the black and white narrative of these times.

Another Fall

The day before Thanksgiving
and my meditation speaks
of forgiveness, its necessity

like a memory I twist
in these blue roots of spruce
this fall day

mourning like every other

my white cat teaches me tenacity
with a bright red string
brought to me again,

away, again, caught
in the trapeze of his gaze
listening for the doves

filling these hours.

Paranoid for Providence

Suspicion, like a snake, sneaks up my back,
whispering, "There is truth to this beauty,
an arc of justice in this world. All this
brokenness just a means to grow and let go."

It takes all my strength to drown it down,
to swipe my phone and count my dislikes.

Yet signs still come to me, secret and subtle,
like the bee tapping persistently outside my window,
distracting my attention, tapping out her code:
there is a grace that prowls in the darkness.

Signs, sudden and startling, like roadside fields
swaying with goldenrod, conspiring against me
and my gloom. Some days I fear
the world is out to get me with its grandeur.

Daniel Flatley

What Is Art

Mary Reynolds switched off the electric kettle in the galley kitchen just off the mansion's main ballroom and dropped two black tea bags into mismatched ceramic mugs, filling them to the brim with hot water and carrying them into the alcove where she had her office. The new CEO of an arts foundation that underwrote several organizations in the Ohio Valley, she had been spending an inordinate amount of time arguing with the director of the Gatehouse Theater about his upcoming production of "Uncle Vanya." He was a small but strident man named Yuriy Andropov, and he was insisting that the play be done in Russian. He said he wanted to preserve the original language and artistic intentions of its author.

After their series of phone conversations had failed to yield a solution, Mary had asked Yuriy to stop by her office to discuss a path forward. Since she expected the meeting to be tense, she had made tea and set out a tray of cookies to help smooth things over. There was no way to accommodate Yuriy's wishes. It was 1975 and you simply couldn't do a play in Russian for a small-town audience; in addition to the political considerations, no one would be able to understand it. So Mary intended to keep the meeting short.

As she rounded the corner to her office, she saw Yuriy sitting in a chair in front of her desk, gazing out the window overlooking the foundation's courtyard. He was wearing a dark turtleneck, a tan corduroy jacket, and a greasy black fisherman's cap even though it was 80 degrees outside. He seemed to be watching the clouds pass over the garden, where they dappled the lilies and orchids and cast shadows on the stolid statues and delicate sundials at its borders, giving them an air of melancholic brilliance.

She handed Yuriy his cup of tea. The theater director took it in his great scarred hands and brought it to his liver-colored lips, which were surrounded by his drooping unshaven jowls. He took one sip and spat the tea all over Mary's desk.

"Bah!" he said, wiping his mouth with the sleeve of his coat. "Too hot!"

Mary watched as the tea soaked into her desk calendar and notes for a presentation to the board of directors scheduled for that afternoon.

"I'm sorry Mr. Andropov," she said. "Would you like some milk for your tea?"

"Yes, yes," Yuriy said. "Milk. And call me Yuriy. We are colleagues, yes?"

"Right," Mary said. "Of course."

"Thank you," Yuriy said. "There's no need to be so formal. Americans. You pride yourselves on being informal. So . . . Be informal!"

"Of course, Mr. Andropov," Mary said before correcting herself. "I mean, Yuriy. I'll be right back."

Mary carried the mugs back to the kitchen where she added some milk to his and a lump of sugar to hers. She returned to her office and put Yuriy's mug down in front of him and took hers behind her desk. She sat, took a long sip, and looked over at her guest, who was staring blankly out the window.

"Mr. Andropov," she said, attempting to break his reverie. She got no reaction.

"Yuriy!" she all but shouted, trying to rouse him.

He started and looked at her with renewed interest.

"What?!" he said, nearly yelling at her, before reaching forward for his mug of tea and taking a sip.

"I wanted to talk to you about the Gatehouse's next production," she said. "I understand you're doing Chekhov?"

"Yes," Yuriy said, taking another sip of tea. "Uncle Vanya. Genius! The best!"

"Absolutely," Mary said, looking at Yuriy carefully. "It is a wonderful play. Certainly one of his best. We are all looking forward to it."

"Yes, yes," Yuriy said with a look of mild annoyance. "You're looking forward to it. I'm looking forward to it. We're all looking forward to it. Is that what you called me here to tell me? That you're 'looking forward to it?'"

"No, Yuriy, not exactly," Mary said, wrapping her hands around her tea mug and choosing her next words carefully. "It's come to my attention that . . ."

"It's come to your attention that what?" Yuriy said, interrupting her.

"It's come to my attention that you're planning to do the play in Russian."

"Yes, of course," Yuriy said, sitting back in his chair and taking a sip of tea.

"Well," Mary said, unsure how to proceed. "Do you think that's a good idea?"

"What do you mean?" Yuriy said.

"Do you think it's a good idea to do the play in Russian? I mean, I don't think there are many Russian speakers here in the Ohio Valley."

"But it is written in Russian," Yuriy said. "It was first performed in Russian. It is Russian!"

"Yes, I realize that," Mary said. "But I'm sure there's a good translation available."

"Bah!" Yuriy said with a dismissive gesture. "No translation can capture the heart of the play, its essence. You would lose the whole meaning."

"Well, I don't know about that," Mary said, changing tactics. "But the simple fact is you cannot do the play in Russian. No one will understand it, Mr. Andropov."

"I told you, call me Yuriy! Are you trying to tell me how to run my theater?"

Mary took a beat here, steeling herself for what might come next. She checked to see that the receptionist was at her desk in the outer office. Seeing that she was, and with the phone near at hand, she continued.

"It's not your theater, Mr. Andropov," she said. "It is funded and administered by the Institute. And the fact is you cannot do the play in Russian. Our mission here is to foster an artistic environment for the community that is welcoming and accessible to all its members. Quite frankly, I fail to see how doing a play in a foreign tongue that no one understands will serve to advance that mission. So that's that. Are we clear?"

She was met with an icy silence, which she soon realized was more terrifying than the physical attack she had been expecting. Yuriy just stared at her. Then he smiled. And that was even more frightening. He threw up his hands in a gesture of supplication.

"Very well, Mrs. Reynolds," he said obsequiously. "We won't do the play in Russian. We don't have to, you know. It's not required, is it? I happen to know of a few serviceable translations. You do lose something in the process, but that can't be helped. We will make it up with superior artistry."

"Very good," Mary said.

"Now, is that all?" Yuriy said.

"Yes."

"I can go?"

"Yes. You can go. Thank you for coming in."

"No," Yuriy said. "Thank you. Good day, Mrs. Reynolds."

"Good day, Yuriy," Mary said.

* * *

That evening, after she had completed all her other tasks, Mary locked her office and walked outside. It was late June, and a warm breeze blew through the garden, carrying the scent of lilacs over the parking lot, where her Plymouth Valiant was one of the few cars remaining. She looked over and recognized the small Mercedes convertible driven by the Institute's chairman and allowed herself a slight smile as she remembered how she'd dealt with his question at the board meeting. She'd assured him the Andropov matter had been handled.

It was going on 7 P.M. and the sky was turning to honey. She fired up the Valiant and drove out of the parking lot and west into the setting sun. She took a back road over the hill toward the farmhouse she was renting with her husband Tom, a young lawyer who'd just joined a practice in town. When she arrived at the house, she found Tom sitting on the porch with a bottle of chilled white wine and a pair of long-stem glasses. She'd phoned him earlier in the day to tell him about her victory with Yuriy.

Tom came to meet her, carrying a small wildflower he must have picked from the field behind their house. He kissed her gently on the forehead and presented her with the flower ceremoniously, congratulating her on her great triumph and leading her by the hand back to the porch where he poured them both a generous portion of wine. They sat there drinking slowly and deeply, watching the sun set over the hills, and went inside for a dinner of Coq Au Vin he had prepared earlier in the evening and left to warm in the oven.

That night they made love on the screened-in porch in back of the house, climaxing together as the weather began to turn cooler and a breeze floated from the ridges beyond the farmhouse, drying the sweat on their backs. Tom whispered to Mary that he loved her, and she felt happy and content, at home for the first time in many months.

The first signs of trouble emerged the following week when Nancy, who in addition to being the Institute's receptionist also acted as Mary's personal secretary, began to receive an odd set of invoices from the Gatehouse's financial manager, a tall, thin man named Gary who also served as the theater's stage manager and house electrician. At first, he had submitted receipts for a pair of overhead projectors—the kind one might use in an elementary or high school setting—and these were approved without much question.

Then Gary began to submit receipts that led both Nancy and Mary to believe he was constructing some sort of elaborate electronic device. He had asked for several hundred small lightbulbs as well as a custom-made mechanical track and a complex system of diodes and transistors that would alternate power according to a pattern set by a rudimentary computer designed by an opera company in Vienna. All told, the items ran to more than $15,000, which was three times the Gatehouse's budget for the year. What was worse, the volume and pace of invoices showed no signs of diminishing. When Nancy came into the office on a Monday morning after the Fourth of July, she found a new pile of invoices, including one for consulting fees for the company that operated a flashing billboard in Times Square.

"Times Square . . . New York?" Mary said as she went through the pile at Nancy's desk.

"That's the one," Nancy said. "And look, here's another one for a financial services company that makes electronic stock tickers."

"What in the world is going on down there?" Mary wondered aloud.

She left the office and drove downtown, stopping first at her doctor's office for the results of some recent tests. She arrived at the Gatehouse around noon. The theater was in a historic district with century-old storefronts across the street and a new modern fire station and parking garage next to it. The building itself was an old church that had been converted about 10 years before, leaving some residents upset that a house of worship had been given over to what they considered the devil's work. She parked her car on the street and headed inside. She entered the first floor, walked past the ticket booth, heard the unmistakable sounds of a set being constructed, and smelled sawdust in the musty air. She walked up the steps to the theater itself and encountered a most extraordinary scene.

Gary and another worker were hoisting a large electronic billboard above the stage using a complex system of ropes and pulleys. Two other men perched atop impossibly tall ladders were fastening the sign into place with electric drills as Yuriy directed the entire effort from a spot in the middle of the theater's seats. "Higher! Higher!" he cried as the men strained to pull the sign into place and wrestled with its unwieldy bulk as they tried to maintain balance on their ladders. "You must go higher! It must be perfect!" Yuriy cried, driving them on.

Meanwhile, on the stage below, actors wandered around with their scripts in their hands, practicing lines. At the edge of the proscenium, a tall man stooped over a portable music stand and worked with some of the actors on their pronunciation of a string of Russian words. Mary recognized the man as a professor of Slavic languages at the local community college. She stood there stunned for a moment or two before marching up to Yuriy and demanding his attention.

"Yuriy!" she shouted at the director, who was still overseeing the effort to install the sign.

Yuriy looked at her briefly and went back to what he was doing. The sign was now in place and the workers were screwing it into the frame. The sound of drills, high and shrill, combined with the cacophony of actors on the stage, made it impossible for Mary to hear her own thoughts, let alone communicate them to someone else. She needed to act, and fast, or the moment would be lost. She left Yuriy to his own devices and walked to the side of the stage where long orange extension cords were plugged into the wall.

She got a firm grip on the plugs and yanked them from the outlet, listening to the sound quickly die away. Her actions, abrupt and decisive as they were, also silenced the actors on stage. Only the professor, who was largely oblivious to the world around him even at the best of times, continued exhorting his pupils. But he quickly fell silent when he looked up from his music stand and saw everyone staring at Mary.

"What are you doing?" Mary shouted at Yuriy, marching back to where he was standing in the middle of the theater.

Yuriy ignored her, staring straight ahead at the stage. He seemed lost in his own thoughts. After a moment passed, he began absent-mindedly chewing on the edge of his thumb. Mary could feel the cast and crew, even the language professor, staring at her. She considered her next words carefully. She had to show them who was boss. As she was thinking of what to say, one of the workers on the ladders nearly lost his balance but caught himself at the last minute. A few screws fell from where he had been holding them between his teeth and bounced off the stage with a sound that echoed throughout the space. Mary was startled for a moment, then repeated her question.

"Yuriy," she said. "What are you doing?"

The director looked at her out of the corner of his eye and waved one of his hands at her dismissively. When he looked again and saw that she had not gone away or cowered in fear, he turned to address her, pulling himself up to his full height and speaking in a slow, measured, and digni-fied manner.

"I am running my theater company," he said. "What does it look like I'm doing?"

"What's all this?" Mary said.

"All what?" Yuriy asked, shrugging his massive shoulders, which were still covered in a heavy coat.

"All this!" Mary said, finally growing exasperated and motioning with her hands and arms to all the activity on the stage: The ladders, the sign, the extension cords, the ropes and pulleys, the actors and tutor.

"That is nothing," Yuriy said. "That is stage management."

"What's the sign for?" Mary said.

Yuriy sighed.

"Translation," he said.

"And the professor?" Mary asked.

"For the Russian," Yuriy said.

"Yuriy," Mary said. "We need to talk."

Yuriy sighed again and covered his eyes with his hand. He stared at the ground in front of him and cursed in Russian.

"Yuriy!" Mary shouted.

"What?!" Yuriy shouted back.

"Can we talk?"

"Yes, yes," Yuriy said. "Take a break, everyone."

There was a great commotion as the actors and workers left their posts. The men on the ladders climbed down. The stage manager gathered up the scripts and led the professor to a place backstage where he could sit. Meanwhile, Mary and Yuriy continued staring at each other in the middle of the theater. The actors and workers gathered on the edge of the stage to watch the scene. Mary was the first to speak.

"I thought we talked about this?" she said.

Yuriy once again made a dismissive gesture with his hand, but when he saw that Mary was standing her ground, he addressed her question.

"Yes," he said. "We talked about this. But I changed my mind."

"What do you mean, you changed your mind?" Mary said. "You can't just do that."

"Of course I can," Yuriy said, his voice rising. "I am an artist. I can do anything I want!"

"You're not an artist," Mary said. "You're a small-town theater director under the employment of the Arts Institute, whose job it is to stage productions that people will understand and enjoy and maybe learn something from."

"And be challenged by?" Yuriy asked.

"Yes, occasionally," Mary said. "Perhaps."

"I would say always, Mrs. Reynolds," Yuriy said. "Always be challenged by."

"How so?" Mary said.

"Let me ask you a question, Mrs. Reynolds," Yuriy said. "What is art?"

"Art is . . ." Mary said before trailing off.

"Yes?" Yuriy said, prodding her.

"That's a ridiculous question," she said.

"Aha!" Yuriy exclaimed. "Only ridiculous because you don't have an answer."

"This is nonsense," Mary said.

"No, no," Yuriy said. "Not nonsense. You are an arts administrator. What is art?"

"I don't have to answer that," Mary said.

"Very well," Yuriy said. "I will tell you. Art is the soul's way of communicating with the eternal. Of slipping the bonds of this feeble, mortal existence and engaging with something beyond human experience."

Mary laughed.

"No, no," Yuriy said. "It's not funny. It's true. And do you know how art begins?"

"Enlighten me," Mary said.

"It begins by shocking the soul out of its malaise. It begins by challenging the mind and the body. It begins with difficulty and is enhanced by challenging material. It begins by reaching for something beyond normal experience."

"Is that so?" Mary said.

"Yes," Yuriy said. "It is."

"That's ridiculous," Mary said.

"It's not," Yuriy said.

"That's why you're doing the play in Russian?" Mary said.

"Yes," Yuriy said. "With translation."

Mary looked at the electronic sign above the stage and at the actors and workers below it.

"That thing will never work," she said.

"It will," Yuriy said.

Mary stared at him. For a moment, she could see his vision—its appeal was made plain to her. The Russian would be a shock to the audience, but the subtitles would guide them through. It would be a novel presentation of a work nearly a century old, making it accessible to a whole new generation without sacrificing any of the artist's original language. It could work; it could be great. But once again Mary became conscious of the eyes of the cast and crew upon her. Hadn't she made her position plain? Hadn't she explained to Yuriy why this could not work? If she gave into his demands now, all would be lost. No one would ever respect her again. She stiffened her spine and addressed him plainly.

"You're fired," she said.

Yuriy laughed.

"You can't fire me," he said.

"Yes, I can," Mary said. "I have the authority."

"No," Yuriy said. "You don't. My contract says I can only be fired by the board of directors."

"Very well," Mary said. "I'll take it up with them. They'll back me up on this."

"You're sure?" Yuriy said.

"Of course I'm sure," Mary said.

"Okay," Yuriy said, sitting down. "We'll wait here. Mary walked back to her car, her fists clenched, her head held high in defiance of Yuriy's intransigence. She fired up the Valiant and drove past the steel mills and warehouses of downtown, through a tunnel and over a bridge until she came to the leafy suburban sprawl of one of the city's wealthier neighborhoods. There, at the top of a small hill, in another converted nineteenth-century mansion, Mary found the law offices of Jim Sullivan, Esq., as well as his sleek convertible parked at the entrance. She maneuvered her oversized vehicle into the firm's small parking lot and turned it off, remembering to put the keys in her purse. She took a few deep breaths and walked inside where she was greeted by a receptionist.

Mr. Sullivan was in a meeting, she was told, and could be tied up for several hours. Having no alternative, and not entirely believing the receptionist, who looked down her nose at her and seemed to regard her as one of those silly young women who didn't wear a bra and had no professional training, she said she would wait. It was getting on toward lunch and she believed the meeting would have to break up at some point so the participants could get something to eat.

At 12:05 P.M., the door to the firm's main conference room opened. A group of young lawyers walked out carrying legal tablets, file folders, and empty containers of coffee. After they all left, a tall, fit-looking man with salt and pepper hair and a neatly trimmed mustache emerged. He wore navy blue pinstripe suit pants, a crisply starched white shirt, and a red silk tie. As he walked out of the room, he bit the end off a long cigar and stuck it between his teeth. He removed a gold lighter from his pants pocket and began playing with it absent-mindedly as he approached the receptionist's desk. He glanced briefly over to where Mary was sitting in an antique ladder-back chair but seemed to take no notice of her. She tried to catch his eye, but it was the receptionist who pointed her out to him when she gave him his phone messages. He came over and greeted her warmly, extending his hand and giving her a wide smile.

"Mrs. Reynolds," he said cheerily. "What a nice surprise. How wonderful to see you."

"It's good to see you too, Jim," Mary said.

"What can I do for you?" Jim said.

"I need to speak with you right away," Mary said. "It's about the Gatehouse."

A look of concern passed over the chairman's face for a brief moment, but he smiled again and said, "Yes, of course. Please come into my office. Can I get you anything? Some coffee perhaps?"

"No thank you," Mary said.

"Very well," he said. "Please follow me."

They walked up the ornate spiral staircase that wound through the center of the mansion, past oil portraits of the firm's previous head partners, and into a comfortable second-floor office that looked out on the town's main thoroughfare. The room was decorated in the federal style with red and beige wallpaper and several landscape paintings. There was an oak desk and a credenza as well as shelves upon shelves of law books behind glass. Mary took a seat at one of the silk upholstered armchairs reserved for visitors and put her purse on the floor beside her. It was her second time in his office and she remembered her first interview with him after she applied for the position. He had been friendly and judicious as he reviewed her credentials and asked her about her artistic philosophy.

She'd won him over on that occasion, despite having less experience than most of the other applicants and hoped to again.

"Do you mind if I smoke?" the chairman asked her, gesturing toward his cigar.

"Please go right ahead," Mary said. "It's your office."

The chairman nodded and walked over to a nearby window, opening it a couple of inches and letting in the noise of the traffic from the street and the smell of the honeysuckle that grew in a planter on the window-sill. He lit his cigar with his gold lighter and took a few contemplative puffs. He tossed the lighter onto his desk and sat back in his chair.

"Now," he said, between puffs on his cigar. "What can I do for you?"

"Well, Mr. Sullivan," Mary began.

"Jim," the chairman said, stopping her.

"Well, Jim," Mary said. "There seems to be an issue with Mr. Andropov, the Gatehouse's director."

"Yes," the chairman said, blowing out a thick stream of smoke. "I know."

"You do?" Mary said, her eyes beginning to water.

"What you have to understand, Mrs. Reynolds," the chairman began.

"Mary," Mary said. The chairman gave a thin smile.

"What you have to understand, Mary, is that Yuriy Andropov has been with us for many years. He's a talented director and a hard worker and he has really made the Gatehouse into what it is today. With someone like that, the board is inclined to give a little latitude. Do you understand what I'm saying?"

"I understand it perfectly well, Mr. Sullivan," Mary said. "But I believe you're making a mistake."

"How so?"

"I thought we agreed that doing the play in Russian was a 'no go,'" Mary said. "Isn't that what we discussed at the board meeting last month? I told Yuriy not to go forward with that plan. I was very clear on that point."

The chairman listened carefully to her argument and appeared to consider its merits for a moment. He tipped his head ever so slightly backward and puffed thoughtfully on his cigar. He looked at the ceiling. The room filled with smoke.

"Yes, well," he eventually said. "As I said before, we're inclined to give Yuriy a little latitude on these matters. After all, he is a political refugee."

"But that was 20 years ago!" Mary said.

"Even so," the chairman said, eyeing her coldly.

"Jim, I'm asking you to please back me up on this," Mary said, a strange tightness in the back of her throat. "It's important that we have a united front."

The chairman considered this for a moment, puffing all the while on his cigar. The window, which was original to the building, slipped a few centimeters down in its frame, closing the gap where the smoke could escape. Mary coughed a couple of times and dabbed at her eyes with some tissues she kept in her purse. At last he spoke.

"How long have you been with us, Mary?" he said.

"About six months."

"I see," the chairman said, rolling the cigar around with his fingers to inspect the label. "My suggestion would be to let this one go."

"How so?" Mary said.

"Don't make this into a bigger issue than it needs to be," the chairman said. "Let's call it a difference of aesthetic interpretation and move on."

"I'm afraid I can't do that," Mary said.

"Why not?" the chairman said, narrowing his eyes ever so slightly. It was becoming hard to see him through the smoke.

"Because," Mary said, struggling to get out her next words through a coughing fit. "Because it would mean the board has no confidence in me. Because it would mean that for the rest of my time here, however long that might be, no one would respect me."

The chairman considered that for a moment as Mary gave in to another coughing fit. He got up and opened the window and stuck a thick volume of West Virginia case law between the sash and the sill. He waved some of the smoke out with his hands and used the intercom to ask the receptionist to bring Mary a glass of water.

"I'm sorry about that," he said, extinguishing his cigar in a heavy crystal ashtray on his desk. "Bad habit."

"That's okay," Mary said as the receptionist handed her a glass of water and opened the door to let some of the smoke escape into the hall.

"I guess I just don't realize how bad it can get in here," he said. "I apologize, really."

"It's okay," Mary said between gulps of water.

"As I was saying," the chairman continued. "I think we should let this one go. Yuriy has really earned himself a lot of goodwill around here over the years. It would be a real shame to have to end things on this note."

"You're serious?" Mary said.

"I'm afraid I am."

"Then I quit," Mary said, standing up to leave.

"Wait," the chairman said. "Wait a minute."

But she was already gone.

* * *

On her way to her car she ran into her husband Tom, who was delivering a box of legal briefs to the chairman's office. Astonished to see her, he asked her to wait for him and told her they could get lunch together.

"I'll see you at home, Tom," she said, moving past him to her car. She fired up the engine and drove straight to their house.

When she got in the front door, she tore off her clothes and headed for the shower. After she'd washed the smell of the cigar smoke out of her hair and off her skin, she started a load of laundry and poured herself a glass of white wine. She sat down at the kitchen table with it and stared at it for a few minutes, trying to decide just how drunk she wanted to get. When she couldn't make up her mind, she poured the wine down the drain, smashed the glass against the sink, cleaned up the shards, and sat down at the table to cry. She was asleep with her head resting on her arms when Tom came home at 6 P.M. with several cartons of food from the city's only Chinese restaurant. She devoured half a container of pork lo mein and several helpings of egg foo young before she felt willing to talk. Tom waited patiently for her to begin.

"I suppose you want to know what happened at Jim's office," Mary finally said, chewing on an egg roll.

"Yes," Tom said gently. "If you feel like talking about it."

"Well, there's not much to say, really," Mary said. "He wouldn't back me up on the Andropov business."

"I know," Tom said.

"You do?"

"Yes," Tom said, pushing at his plate nervously. "I spoke with him."

"You 'spoke with him?'" Mary said. "When did you speak with him?"

"I had to drop off some stuff for him from my boss," Tom said. "Some case they're working on together."

"Right," Mary said.

"Well," Tom continued. "He invited me into his office. Offered me a cigar."

"Oh God."

"I know," Tom said. "I didn't accept. Anyway, he told me about the whole thing."

"What 'whole thing,'" Mary said.

"Just that you guys had had a fight about the play Andropov was doing, some Chekhov thing, and that he wanted to do it in Russian, and you didn't."

"Jesus!" Mary exclaimed. "First of all, it wasn't a fight; it was a discussion. And secondly, that asshole wouldn't back me up because he's got no balls."

"Yes," Tom said, clearing his throat. "Well, that's what we talked about."

"It must have been a great conversation!"

"Mary," Tom said, raising his voice for the first time in their marriage. "Jim Sullivan is one of the best lawyers in this town. His firm takes in three, four times what we do in a month. And haven't you told me that he's always been fair?"

"Yes!" Mary said. "But he's a ball-less asshole with shit for brains!"

"That's just not true," Tom said.

A few moments of silence passed between them. Tom pushed his plate of food away, and Mary dropped the egg roll she'd been eating. She fixed her husband with a cold stare.

"Whose side are you on?" she said.

"I'm not on anyone's side," he said. "I just think . . ."

"Aha!" Mary said, getting up from the table. "You just think what? That your wife's a shrew? An unreasonable female? Too emotionally wrapped up in the case? What, Tom? What is it?"

"Nothing," Tom said. "I just think you might want to consider things from the board's point of view, that's all. Not do anything rash."

"Oh great," Mary said, standing at the sink. "Thanks for all the support."

"Mary, I'm sorry," Tom said, coming up behind her to give her a hug. She felt the warmth of his body and allowed his arms to encircle her waist, but when he tried to turn her toward him, she resisted, keeping her shoulders square with the sink and concentrating on the patterned backsplash above it. She'd spent the last several hours being pushed about by men, really the past several weeks or even months. Even when they were out of her sight, they were moving against her. The next move would be her own. Whatever decision she would make would be hers and hers alone.

Later that night, after Tom had showered and gone to bed, Mary poured herself another glass of wine and sat at the kitchen table. From her purse, she removed an item and placed it next to the glass. She stared at them both. She stared at the doctor's note until the lines blurred together. Pregnant. She took a sip of wine, savoring the crisp cool flavor of the chardonnay, tasting the dark, oaky finish, and poured the rest of the glass down the sink.

Several weeks later, toward the end of September, as the days were growing shorter and the nights cooler, and the sound of football helmets crashing against each other could be heard throughout the valley, the Gatehouse Theater staged its season opening performance of "Uncle Vanya" under longtime company director Yuriy Andropov. The play was performed in Russian with real-time translation via a specially designed billboard system that flashed dialogue from multiple angles in the theater simultaneously. It was a resounding success. Alerted to the unusual nature of the performance, a Pittsburgh theater critic made her way down from the city to review the production. Her notice, which was full of praise for the performances, the staging, and the dramaturgy, attracted the attention of the chief theater critic for the New York Times, who flew in for a weekend of performances. In the following week's Sunday arts section of the paper was a two-page spread about the Gatehouse's production, which the chief critic heralded as nothing less than the second coming of American regional theater. The run of "Uncle Vanya" was extended by several weeks to accommodate all the interest.

Throughout this heady period, Andropov was as magnanimous in victory as he had been defiant in defeat. He heaped praise upon the Art Institute, including its CEO Mary Reynolds, whom he singled out for her steadfast devotion to the arts. Mary graciously accepted the praise and told a reporter that she had tried to support the artist in whatever way he needed though they'd had their disagreements. Of paramount importance to her was the accessibility of the work, she explained, but it was also necessary to challenge the audience at times and Yuriy's vision had balanced those feats quite nicely. There were rumors that she had threatened to quit unless the tight-fisted board of directors agreed to provide the funding for the production but these she dismissed with a wave of her hand, saying only, "The board has always been supportive of our programs."

The Gatehouse's production of "Uncle Vanya" had its final performance on an October night near Halloween. People came from all around to see it, including from as far away as New York and California. They packed into the Gatehouse's small theater, a capacity crowd of 300. Some stood the whole time, and Jim Sullivan had to slip the fire marshal $100 to ignore the violation. The final curtain call was met with a twenty-minute standing ovation, and Mary and her husband Tom were in the front row clapping right along with the crowd and beaming with pride.

As the theatergoers left the venue that night and looked down the street toward the Court Street movie house, they saw a line of would-be patrons that stretched around the block, awaiting admittance to a new feature-length production by a young director who was setting

Hollywood ablaze. The film's story was ridiculous—something about a demon shark that was hunting human victims off the coast of a fictitious New England Island—but the artistry of the film was said to be masterful, elevating what was essentially a "B" movie to new heights. Even more remarkable was how commercially successful it was proving to be, packing moviegoers across the country in for several showings a day. Some were even returning for repeat viewings.

It was just such a pair of repeat customers that Mary and Tom happened to overhear as they got into their Valiant for the drive home. Two young men, barely out of high school, were standing toward the end of the line and having an animated conversation about the film. The context of the conversation seemed to be about how innovative the staging and cinematography were, particularly when it came to revealing the shark at the heart of the story. Mary paused to listen for a moment before getting into the car.

"The way they waited until the end to show the shark," one of the young men said. "That was brilliant."

"Yes," the other one said. "Pure genius."

Mary laughed as they pulled away from the curb, marveling at how random the universe was in its bestowing of artistic grace.

Their Lovemaking Was Like

Their lovemaking was like
the rain

in August when the grass burns
brown and dry,

yet sometimes it was an April
thunderstorm that rocked the house,

other times like the dew,
falling without notice
or effort and gone
just as quick.

but mostly it was like
a steady mist
gently falling and sinking
into the welcoming ground
leaving the thirsty land lush
and verdant.

Portrait of the Beloved with Rain

Where her skin molts, light struggling through water, I linger with the quick flesh behind her neck.

Today, I saw ice in the shape of her shoulder blades hanging from a log above a riffle. Tonight, as my tongue finds that cold again, I shiver at the body's dullness betraying its name.

Her legs are corded like running sap from a gash on a maple's bark, her stomach the glide in a river clean enough that I eat the fish and lay in the current until the sky is so full of stars I can't find my way to shore.

The hair on her upper lip is frost on the leaves of lamb's ear that I kiss and kiss until my face is wet.

My beloved does with me
what rain does with streams.

Eight Attempts at Connection

1.
The trees drop their color
and the air tastes of altitude
ripe with wingbeat and squawks.

2.
The leaf meets
the surface of the water,
and they become one.

3.
My blood is a river
that circles and circles,
always in search of an ocean.

4.
I want to love you
the way the waves love the earth
into dust.

5.
Sumac sets the hills ablaze
but the fire inside me
has no audience.

6.
I dream of eating
an eyelash and carrying you
with me forever.

7.
Once brought to a rotary phone,
I could not understand
how to summon a greeting.

8.
We speak only in postcards,
each hand inking the paper
then pushing it away.

Sandra Kolankiewicz

Give Me Black

I was a little too dark for him, and
        I don't mean skin, though he was not too
dark for me. We had plenty of light, in
        fact barely escaped all the happiness
surrounding us, the tourists spending too
        much, knowing nothing of what was said of
them in another language, Mass the same
        in any country, five stud poker games
following the rules we all know, the bread
        on the table recognizable no
matter where we supped, whether the sky was
        blue or grey. The air was white when we met,
which meant we had nothing to compare to,
        not one of our colors absorbed. Give me
black any day, saturated with the
        rainbow, complete and heavy with spectrum.

Steubenville, 1819

After Louis Legrand Noble

I.

As, happy in the company of ancients
who leechlike to their fainting master
clung, Blake was crawling from hiatus
to Jerusalem, his last hot Hell along
the Strand, Thomas Cole caught this
hill-face unwrinkled with after-coke
and learned here to use his landing
oils. That August, sedge grass and
wild chive like the county's eyelash
parted and bunched about his boot
shafts, brooming off wafers of mud
from one muddy spring after another
—Lancaster, York, Bedford, Somerset:
commons and familiars strung out of
Philadelphia—he choked his famous
fluting for a cross and pushed upon
a goblet golden and sanguine as any
Keats, sprinting through his only
spring, had oded to. Top lip of our fat
plateau, plenty running over to feed
this collar of Ohio: we can barely
dig the promise that it swelled with.

II.

Or chaffy grain beneath the thresher's flail:
—Samuel Taylor Coleridge

Two years of what rapture! lonesome
and proleptic, Theban shadowbox of
house and head—and Cole was down-
Valley and trying West, the dirt meters
of old Ebenezer's Trace underfoot from
where it grabbed at the Ferry bank to
Zanesville. This was a child's pilgrim-
age, stippled with firsts, and to a city
shrouded in brief centrality, unspired
by a century still, its little Rome-top
razed to the modern mind. So, tavern
to tavern he found whole crews brushed
and outlined, their lust for likeness sated,
and that in a Panic only likeness sold. Vain
pursuit! —and it panged him back to risk
a darkened river, tipped him green into
the rapid, spit him up a praying man . . .

North and Washington, a riprap of boat-
yard and foundry steeled sidewheelers for
port at Apalachicola. Inland, sheep drifted
fleecy and mill-less from a fire unfaded,
yet prepared to fade. And family vernals
emptied out to Allegheny and enterprise.

Office Ladies

A is for Audrey, who sniffles all day.
B is for Barb, who negotiated her pay.
C is for Cindy, the de facto nurse.
D is for Dot, with the flask in her purse.
E is for Eunice, who eats at her desk.
F is for Francie, who dances burlesque.
G is for Gudrun, imported to last.
H is for Holly (legendarily fast).
I is for Iris and the florals she'd waft.
J is for Jami, impeccably coiffed.
K is for Kelly, perpetually cold.
L is for Lauren, not young and not old.
M is for Mae, who is power-adjacent.
N is for Nina, who's sadly complacent.
O is for Ondine, who sneaks naps in her car.
P is for Paula, the one who'll go far.
Q is for Quinn (for sure, somebody's kid).
R is for Rhonda's lost Tupperware lid.
S is for Sally of the unsilenced phone.
T is for Tate, always good for a loan.
U is for Ursula's hidden magazines.
V for Veronica with her Lean Cuisines.
W for Winnie of the stairwell walks.
X is for Xenia, who watches the clock.
Y is for Yolanda and her poker face.
Z is for Zelda, who'll inherit the place.

Why We Get Tired of the Home We Know and Don't See

Look for it in a bramble thuggery
fencing a sloping field post-burn:

You can't carry it.
You tell no one.
You get to kick the first
    word you've heard too much:

        mountain   mawmaw
        cabin   river
        opioid   welfare
        trailer   unemployed
        mines   Mountain Dew

Furnace hunger denuded the hills
in this county known for trees—
100 years ago not a   single tree
left standing over   all the hills.

You tell no one.
    Sentences—not big ones.
Noun verb like left right.
You can always walk too far.

Our reticence
grew. Furnaces cooled.
We learned again to hide valleys.
To hide our ground.
Keep the pillagers at bay.

You can't carry it.
Where do you put a flag to mark
        the middle of nowhere?

Some words:
        Indigenous sounds like a tree.
        Itinerant like ignorant.
        Ignorant like indigent.
        Indigent like beaten.
                Beaten like eaten like elite.

~~the last destruction was the fire in the mines, the smoke beneath~~
        ~~our homes~~
~~the last destruction was the turnpike that left us forgotten~~
~~the last destruction was the highways blasted through ridges~~
~~the last destruction was the valley flooded, a lake for tourists~~
~~the last destruction was NAFTA and the gutting of factories~~
~~the last destruction was the towers for cellular~~
~~the last destruction was Obama~~
~~the last destruction was the wind turbines~~
~~the last destruction was the opioids~~
~~the last destruction was immigrants~~

destruction is the Appalachian refrain.

You get to kick
        the first word
heavy as a stone.
Tell no one you broke
        your toe, your stride.
You get to kick
        every broken branch:

                farm-to-table   ginseng
                artisan   tourism

trails	Chamber of Commerce
resort	manufacturing
distillery	development
generations	rural voters
broadband	mountain bike

Tell no one what you might trust.
    Wonder what you might trust.
Find the words that add up.
    One syllable for each gas station
with pumps dry, prices still dusty and set
    with a figure starting with one.

Look for it in a bramble thuggery
fencing a sloping field post-burn:

destruction is our Appalachian refrain.

Pearls Before . . .

In my Omicron delirium I read the news today.
A 57-year-old man has been given the heart of a pig
for the first time ever. "I know it's a shot in the dark,
but it's my last choice," he said.

Another story reveals that in 1988 he'd stabbed
a 22-year-old man 7 times, leaving him paralyzed
in a wheelchair for the next 19 years till the stabbed
man had a stroke, then died a week shy of his 41st birthday.

Meanwhile, in Israel, in the Negev desert, scientists
have trained goldfish to drive a vehicle on land.
"It goes without saying that fish, in general, are not
naturally equipped to explore terrestrial environments,"
they say. The fish navigate toward a target on the wall
in exchange for food pellets . . .

A knock at the door, I tip delivery driver extra well
as he hands over my glazed pork belly with toasted
garlic, sweet soy, jicama-peanut slaw. As he turns
to go, I swear I catch a glimpse of pulsing gill
through blue surgical mask, then he is gone,
pulling away in his 1997 Honda Accord
with balding tires and rusty exhaust.

The Day Before

Morning is warm bed and cold floor.
Bacon.
Words spoken and unspoken
Move around and through.

Daylight warms the porch,
The pasture,
The book in your hands.

Poems float in rising air.
Hawks hover above them,
Devour them
Like the day devours you.

Afternoon is cut grass and gasoline,
Sweat, high sun.
Clouds lean down.
Shadows play.
Birds laugh and move on.

Poet says, "Light is ivory."
You smile.
Poets know light has color.

It is easy to sit on the swing,
Wait for friends
You know will come.

Blue unburdens the sky
Deeper and deeper
In low slant light
Of early October evening.

Things settle.
Birds.
Daylight.
Words.
You.

In gentle fields
Buck deer browse unhurried.
Poems fall down,
Lead you past the ridge
Toward planets rising,
Moon following across
Unrhymed clouds.

The book,
Still open,
Trembles.

Night wanders in,
Sits on the swing beside you,
Sighs.

Way Ablaze

Nothing strays at night, as if each long stretch
        without sun were the same holiday eve,

everyone content because something good
        has just happened or is about to, the

neighborhood lit up, windows full of folks
        going house to house, the openness that

comes with being naïve, the assumptions
        that accompany privilege, everyone

knowing how to sing, each family with
        at least one member who plays piano.

Let's have a song after dinner, and we
        sing, four generations, as we've always

done, just three television stations in
        a box, the phone attached to the wall on

a short cord, and afterwards chasing and
        flopping in the snow, sledding down the long

front hill under the stars, the Milky Way
        ablaze, so bright it calls even the old

ones out into the cold yard with their canes
        to meet the vastness of the universe.

Gabriel Welsch

Cross Street, Mifflin and 14th, Central Pennsylvania

A student returning to Azerbaijan
kissed the door frame goodbye,
backlit by the snowy tableau
of the railroad street by the Italianate manse

built by Irish carpenters when the trains
started stopping in 1911. He kissed this home
just feet away from the Mennonite women
hunching by Haitian art while a Gullah trio

on CD played contrapuntal "Winter Wonderland."
This land, yours, ours, lives in the incipient gaze
of the perpetually arriving. None of us have lived
everywhere but we have walked elsewhere,

settled in places where even with limitless
horizons, we scarcely understand vastness.
How miserly the provincial pride,
the lifers, the generations

in one place, weaving refusal as virtue.
The Russian woman tends the bake sale
for the volunteer firefighters. Chinese students
ask if they hand her the right number of bills.

On Diwali, the caterer passes the courthouse
and coasts up Mifflin, lost but for GPS, the turn
of the earth leading him to the light,
where a man leans into a doorway a final time.

Perilune

per·i·lune noun *The point at which an object in lunar orbit is
closest to the Moon and experiences the maximum pull of its gravity*

It was the end, less a week, of a very bad year. In April, King was
murdered and cities burned. The President, dragged down by the deaths
of 300 American boys a week in the jungles, and lifespan actuarial tables
unmoved by even his considerable gifts of persuasion, chose to change
for his few remaining years his riverview of history from the Potomac to
the Pedernales. When summer came and was wallowing in the sweltering
fullness of August, cops beat hell out of hippies in Chicago. By autumn
there was a new president in waiting with a secret plan to end the war
and an enemies list.

Now, in winter, on the eve of Christmas 1968, three American war-
riors circled sixty miles above the magnificent desolation of the Moon.
Their vehicle, an improved model of the craft that had incinerated three
friends twenty-two months earlier, still carried the rank tang of cabin
flotsam that, according to every NASA protocol, should have remained
inside the Mission Commander. Soho bookies gave odds of success for
the mongrel Apollo 8 mission cobbled together in five weeks no better
than even money. Nevertheless, the martial crew, with the flinty gaze of
airborne raptors, planned in their ten lunar orbits to prove that the best
right stuff was made in America, recapitulate the cosmology of the Old
Testament to the largest audience to ever hear a human voice, and so
poke a space-suited finger in the eye of the Russian bear.

The house, a Sears & Roebuck Fullerton kit—three main rooms
downstairs and up with a full front porch—sat in the flood plain of a
minor tributary of the Ohio, a colloquial "crick," the coal gob-coated
flow of which resembled liquid copper. It was built in 1929 suddenly and
with some desperation when the family, then seven, was ejected during
an ugly miner's strike from their coal camp bungalow in Hunkie Hollow

into a looming worldwide Depression. It was advertised at $2,185 cut and fitted. Still, according to the meticulous accounting kept by the family's mother, the addition of a back-porch pump and construction finishing costs brought the final price to $3,125.69.

The home remained in the family until after the millennium. Then, after a dying late summer hurricane churned up the Appalachian foothills, astonishing twenty-six souls with sudden mostly watery deaths and filling the house to above the dining room table with creek overflow, it went to a neighbor. Sold as is, warped china cabinet, basement with a ruined batch of homemade dandelion wine, and a ravaged dirt-floor garage that sheltered a cherry 1958 Oldsmobile Holiday Sedan; red over cream with white sidewalls.

This night was the house's thirty-ninth Christmas Eve and thirty-eighth Polish Wigilia celebration. While Christmas 1944 with two sons sweltering on Pacific flecks of coral and jungle and a son-in-law in a soldier's grave in Italy warranted little festivity, the recovery from that year was energetic, reflecting the inherent optimism of still fresh Americans. The house witnessed sons safely home from Armageddon, steady blue-collar toil, and "Polski wesele" marriage celebrations with bread and salt and polkas and the marathon bridal dance. By Christmas Eve 1968 a Fibonacci series of tow-headed grandchildren swelled the multitude at the house's primary and satellite dining tables to nineteen.

For Poles, including American transplants, Christmas Eve is fasting then feasting. The Wigilia banquet begins at the appearance of the first star. On this night it was heralded by two young sisters shivering and hungry from their half hour of searching the darkening firmament above B&B Custom Butchers on the National Road, bursting from the back porch into a steaming wall of Christmas dinner fragrances and announcing, "The star has come!"

After a prayer by the family patriarch, in Polish and always including John L. Lewis and the United Mine Workers in the blessing, the feast commenced. First, the breaking of the round oplatek Christmas wafers at each table setting, divided and shared among all with wishes of thanksgiving and affection and common aspirations for good fortune in the New Year. Next the traditional dishes: borscht and herring in cream from Slobicki's on the Island for the purists; and mild baked carp for grandchildren and other gastronomical delicates. And for everyone pirogi dumplings stuffed with mushrooms or cabbage, vegetable salad, plaited Jewish Challah bread, and finally gingerbread pierniki.

With the gingerbread came the ritual of "małe pisklęta," the "little chicks." With the family crowded into the dining room, every grandchild chose from a sideboard a small glass from a poor family's eclectic suite of stemware and joined a line forming in front of the Grandfather. Their dziadek looked each grandchild up and down in turn then slowly poured a mixture of plum slivovitz brandy and water into each glass and patted each blonde head. The ratio of rosy to clear liquid in the glass represented the patriarch's irrefutable assessment of where the child's journey to adulthood stood for that year. When all the glasses were full the patriarch smiled broadly, told them they were all "good little chicks" and led the chorus of the "Wesołych Świąt" Christmas toast.

In the unenlightened era of gender roles and responsibilities of even the late 1960's, the post-dinner table dispersion found the ladies clearing and washing and drying and the gentlemen retiring to the evergreen scented living room where the grandfather distributed shots of Four Roses bourbon. The little chicks stoically submitted to the interminable duration of this final prelude to the night's essential purpose of opening Christmas presents. They squirmed, exasperated by irrelevant delays that included long-distance phone calls from extended family outposts in rust belt metropolises and the men trooping coatless into the chill night to inspect an uncle's new '69 Buick Riviera.

Finally, the gifting commenced. For the children a matching pair of combination transistor radios and makeup cases, a lapidary stone key chain, and a battery-powered and wired electric puppy that barked and did backflips. For the adults, cufflinks, a car coat with wooden barrel buttons, cartons of Chesterfield Kings, boxes of favored chocolates, and amber bottles of spirits of middling quality.

Then the television was alive, and the screen showed a grayscale image of what looked like a slowly rotating shard of the dinner's oplatek wafer but dusty grey, scored, and pockmarked. When the caption "LIVE TV TRANSMISSION FROM APOLLO 8" appeared, the puppy backflips were halted, shot glasses set down, and children shushed into obedient silence. The room filled with astronauts' crackling radio voices acquainting their transfixed worldwide audience with the Moon's topography as it swam ashen and dusty beneath their oddly shaped viewing portals.

"We are now approaching lunar sunrise, and for all the people back on Earth, the crew of Apollo 8 has a message that we would like to send to you.
'In the beginning God made heaven and earth . . .'"

The grandfather, a fugitive seeker from a dot of a village in the shadow of the Carpathian Mountains, abandoned his tribe's thousand years of peasantry, the last hundred scraping the dirt for Austrian dupeks with delusions of empire. He followed the North Star and the iron trail of German railroads to a ship to Ameryka there to join ten thousand other Bohunks and rednecks in the democratic coal fields of the Appalachian foothills. There also to find a prospect for a new family and home and in the spring the perfume of onions, beets, and cabbages from a patch he scraped for himself.

His was an America of miracles. He spent his forty years of sunless winter weeks underground and emerged mostly whole with only the universal miner stigmata of perpetually black fingertips and lungs. His beloved wife and all their children still lived, and they had their own brood of happy "male piskleta." He could vote for any Democrat he wished and purchased with his Social Security stipends a Zenith Model 5430 color television which every Saturday brought him Gunsmoke and live professional wrestling from Pittsburgh. For these American blessings he put out the flag at least seven times each year, was invariably waiting in his best suit when his polling station opened in years divisible by two, and lit a candle every Sunday to the Black Madonna at St. Joseph's in Wolfhurst.

But this fuzzy television image and assertions there were Americans circling the faraway Moon sorely strained his stolid peasant skepticism.

Yet, this was the season of signs and mysteries, and America was their home. So he raised his glass to the TV screen and chose to append, at least provisionally, this marvel to his list of New World wonders.

"'And God separated light from dark . . .'"

The father, a veteran of Great Depression soup lines and Pacific Theater of Operations chow lines was a believer. A believer that the American revolutionary science and precision engineering of twenty-three Augusts previous, which fashioned Oriental days with a fatal second sunrise and for him a near-term future, were the best way, truth, and life this side of Heaven. He understood also that this saving atomic sword had a Janus side where rockets sending humans to serene space could also bring holocaust arcing inbound.

But it was Christmas Eve, and this remarkable feat being broadcast to the world held some promise. Maybe winning a moon race with the Reds would keep the rockets arcing only upward. And maybe a country rich enough to sponsor a Christmas tale from the Moon could keep his factory running for another twenty years. And maybe the opportunities of the world of science and engineering could keep his clever son from becoming another jungle statistic. This blessing, too, had its reverse side; the siren song that would inevitably lure his son to a distant "center" or "facility" of which there were none along the minor tributaries of the Ohio. For this year at least, the blessings were untainted, and he hoped more than believed that when their darker facets were revealed, he would be able to accept them.

"'and God saw that it was good.'"

The son, a dreamer oldest son of an oldest son, was also the lucky seventh in the sequence of grandchildren. Wired for prose but seduced by science he struggled this autumn with thermodynamics, the plays of ancient Greece, and another dose of Jesuit educational rigor.

He had watched three days earlier, before the trek to his college's Christmas break, $1.60 an hour, work-study job in a third-hand Dodge with a balky push button transmission, the fiery levitation from a tropical launch pad of the most complex machine ever constructed. And, after a stint of scraping chewing gum from women's dorm tables, he had slipped away to view the television broadcast of the first humans to travel to a place influenced by a different celestial body.

Now in this grainy TV transmission from another world, he could see a dream becoming real. It was not yet that summer's cinema vision of pristine business class jaunts to lunar colonies and a psychedelic deep space voyage to Jupiter's black monolith scored by Strauss and Khachaturian. This was sweaty, cramped, porthole views of pallid dirt and craters accompanied by Buck Owens on a floating cassette recorder. And although oblivious of the image buried in an astronaut's film canister, a color tourist photo of a tiny blue marble Earth rising over a desolate lunar horizon that would forever change the planet's understanding of itself, the son felt what he was watching was significant.

And so he decided. He expected that he would never be able to achieve the better ranks of the technical visionaries who generated this night's practical transcendence. But he believed that with effort and blessing and a respectable command of Newton's laws of motion and English synonyms he might contribute, and that the effort was worth making.

"And from the crew of Apollo 8, we close with good night, good luck, a Merry Christmas, and God bless all of you, all of you on the good Earth."

At the end of night's celebration when the grandparents shivered on their full front porch and saw their brood off for the evening, the Moon had already set over Two-Mile Hill, one of the few easy passages, though steep and long, up from the poisoned creeks that leaked and flooded into another Appalachian river. Still in orbit, the Apollo 8 astronauts awaited the critical engine burn that would, by God's grace and the slide rules of NASA engineers, nudge them home to the good Earth.

When the Moon rose again on Christmas afternoon *The Nautical Almanac* calculated that it would not be a new moon but rather a crescent waxing towards full. But for the Son and the Father and the Grandfather for that Christmas and for future Yules, the Moon would remain new, transfigured by three Christmas visitors from a troubled planet at the end of a very bad year.

Jackie

The First Lady shared, later, that the late President said,
and these were then his last words: *Lose the sunglasses.*

This before she saw her life as an ugly, exposed wound.
In the Zapruder film and, consequently, forever and ever.

For all intents and purposes, Jackie was under fire herself
while scrambling onto the back of a limo in that pink suit.

And what but anger at liberties bullets take with a head
would summon a woman to want to protect a man who,

until that day, routinely crooned show tunes in a boat he
made answer the whims of wind and tide? LBJ flanked

Jackie during his swearing in on Air Force One, a hand
raised. In photographs, she hasn't changed clothes, Mrs.

Kennedy, as if we are broken and either mourn or lie in
the belly of a jet dividing the golden hour with its wings.

I'll say it again: No one knew if the shooting had finished
when she got up from where she sat and did all she could.

Clyde

Clyde and I reached the staging area just before dawn. It was a cold night for July. Forty-eight degrees. We waited with the Subaru idling, heater on, windows cracked.

The Bluestone Baptist Church in Jumping Branch, West Virginia, was across the street from Broomstraw Road. Up that road a little way was the holler where, in a house built by her great grandfather, lived Leeann Muklowe, her husband John, their infant daughter Tracy, and their son Jeremiah.

The home had been carved from the surrounding forest and placed with the mountainside directly east, five miles from its back door. The front yard, clear-cut in harvesting the lumber for the house, abutted the state road.

Yesterday, John had gone to work.

It was just before dinner time when Jeremy and his mother and sister returned from their visit to John Henry Historical Park in Talcott, West Virginia. The sun was shining, the day cloudless. His mother pulled down the window shades. The three of them lay down for a nap.

His mother awoke and patted the bed beside her, "Jeremy." Not there. "Jeremy." She raised the blinds. Pulled open the curtains. She looked outside from window after window. Inside under the beds. Checked every room. She opened the closet doors, cabinet doors, even the refrigerator door. Every door. "Wherewherewhere?"

She found his jacket on the coat rack. The back door was unlatched. *At least he's wearing his shoes.* She slammed the door and ran. Clockwise then counterclockwise around the house yelling his name. She stopped to listen and heard the baby crying from inside.

High above, a piercing whistle sounded from a circling broad-winged hawk. Even his eyes would catch no sign of the boy.

Jeremiah "Jeremy" Muklowe. Almost 8 years old. 38 inches tall. 57 pounds. Brown hair and brown eyes.

Was gone.

Leeanna called her husband at work. The UMW shut down the shift at the mine and sent their local members over to join the search. Even the rural letter carrier, Tammy Camaletti, curtailed her deliveries, parked her old jeep Cherokee by all the other vehicles in the Muklowe's front yard, and joined the search.

Behind their home was a gentle slope. A patch of grass led to a scruffy cover of mountain laurel, wild grapevines, thorns, and sticker bushes. Farther on, white oak and beech were scattered among balsam fir, red spruce, and mountain ash. Here and there several stumps remained where hardwood had been cut for the stove.

The slope ended at a dry creek bed. Across the creek was a hill that steepened quickly into a mountain ridge. Several boulders had let loose and rolled into the creek bed.

The searchers walked an arm's length apart, as best they could, all the way to the bottom of the mountain. They flushed three ruffed grouse and spotted a fox. They found a crinkled bag of Mister Bee Potato Chips stuck on a greenbrier vine and a flattened empty 8-ounce Tyler Mountain plastic water bottle. They found old deer and coyote tracks hardened into the mud. No child-size footprints. No sign of the boy.

At dusk, they headed back to the house trailed by a lone striped skunk.

The sheriff called the search off until dawn.

Tammy waited at the house for the search to start the next morning. Her jeep was locked. The undelivered mail, still inside.

She and Leeanna spent the night outside, wrapped in an afghan. Propped in the corner where the deck railing met the back wall, they smoked cigarettes and stared into the night. The lights from inside blazed out in rectangles. Tammy dozed.

Leeanna watched the grey cigarette smoke waft in the light, jostle against the darkness, and disappear. She twirled her hair through the fingers of her right hand and moved her lips in prayer. She stood up, called out, and waited. Listened and called out again. Gave up and sat back down, slumped against the back door. Then she stood back up again.

The sensor light turned on when Leeanna paced and off again after she settled. Then on again when she got up to walk a little ways into the darkness.

Leeanna's husband, out front of the house, doing the same. An echo of sound and light.

* * *

Clyde and I got the call from the Summers County Sheriff yesterday evening after the search was halted for the day.

As we waited for Sheriff Hunlay in the church parking lot, I huddled in the driver's seat with the wool collar of my jacket snapped tight against my neck. Clyde dozed curled up in the back seat.

The boy was believed to be wearing denim pants and a navy blue WVU sweatshirt with "Start em Young Raise em Right" and the WVU logo in gold. White sneakers. I stared into the darkness around the churchyard as if the boy were already there but just waiting to be spotted. Hide-and-seek. Ally, Ally, In Free.

I got out of the truck and walked around. The cornerstone of the current church building dated 1915. A plaque noted that the original church building burned to the ground in 1862 when the Union Army marched through Jumping Branch.

At the time, this was still the western part of Virginia. Yet to become West Virginia. Yet to join the Union.

Were the soldiers roused to anger by a symbol of Christianity residing in a Confederate state? Dedicated abolitionists galled by the white steeple that set like a fresh ax cut against the darkness of the Flat Top Mountain range.

For our God is a consuming fire.

I looked up at the cross as its shape blotted black against the bright whiteness of the waning crescent moon. I looked down from the light to the darkened red brick and the shadowed ground.

"Shovel them under and let me work . . . I am the grass I cover all."

But not enough. Even trampled down and covered up, some things still seep through. Some trace can still be found.

The church's marquee board, encased in brick, rested on a pedestal. White metal framed a glass cover over black felt. White letters pressed onto the felt. The weak light inside the frame barely reached the tops of the letters of the last line that had been added yesterday.

Luke 19:10
For the Son of Man came to seek and to save the lost.
Pray for Jeremy

I got back in the car. "There're a lot of dangers out there that could harm the boy," I said. "We have to get to him first."

Clyde stirred but didn't comment.

* * *

Clyde was a pure-bred bloodhound. Four years old now and one hundred and twenty pounds. He measured a little over two feet from the ground to his shoulders and if he stood on his hind legs his front paws could reach my shoulders. He was tan underneath with a full blanket black coat. Take a can of black paint, pour it out from neck to tail over a tan dog with just enough paint so that it pooled above his paws. That would be Clyde.

Me. I'm a mixed breed. I just turned fifty. I weigh in at one hundred and ninety-six pounds, ten pounds over my wrestling weight in college. I stand just over six feet. My hair has more gray than brown.

Never had a dog before.

* * *

Before I met Clyde, I was a West Virginia State Trooper. I had been assigned to Troop 2, Charles Town Detachment, District 1 for 22 years.

I was working the 7 P.M. to 7 A.M. shift one June 20th. It was West Virginia Day. The state holiday celebrating West Virginia's 1863 admission to the Union as the 35th State. The state formed from several northwestern counties of Virginia that voted to secede from Virginia, after Virginia seceded from the United States in 1861. Virginia would return as a state in 1870 but would not regain the part that had become West Virginia during the American Civil War.

At 2:30 A.M. it came across my radio as a 10-59 "Interview a Witness" from a 911 operator. The address was a house in Orgas, named after the 1919 Orange Gas Coal Company, along the Coal River.

I approached the house with flashing lights, no sirens. I angled the Ford Crown Vic Police Interceptor on the front lawn. The front door was propped open. The porch window was raised halfway up, and the curtains drifted in and out with the breeze. All the downstairs lights were on. The blue strobe bounced against the front of the house and into the entryway, heralding my arrival. I walked up on the porch and could see the woman at the end of the hallway holding the handset of the kitchen wall phone, her face darkened with bruises. Her other hand trembling, holding a steak knife out in front of her face. I stepped into the house. "Tell them I'm here," I called to her.

A chair scraped across the floor and a man stepped into the hallway just in front of the woman, then he turned and walked quickly toward me. I could see his hands; the knuckles were scraped and bloody.

"Officer," he said.

"It's Trooper," I said.

He said something else, but I wasn't listening. I grabbed the handle of my revolver pulled it from its holster and raised the gun high and brought the barrel down on his head. He dropped to his knees. The blood flashed black in the blue emergency lights. I slapped the barrel across his jaw, and he went down to the ground on his side.

The woman had not moved but still held the phone. "Tell them to send an ambulance," I said.

I was placed on administrative leave at the end of my shift.

* * *

Two weeks later, I was sitting on the wooden steps of the front porch of our home in Horse Creek Junction, Boone County. Waiting for the mailman. If you looked across the road and past the windbreak of trees and the small lake, you could see the hills. The old mountains. Worn down.

I watched as a car pulled up. In the sun, the high gloss of the gold roof and navy-blue body stunned my eyes. It was Colonel Slaton, superintendent of the West Virginia State Police in his brand-new Ford Explorer Police Interceptor.

The Colonel said, "You didn't give your commander much choice after what you told the captain from professional standards."

I nodded.

"You told him you buffaloed the suspect. Buffaloed? In the manner of Wyatt Earp in order to apprehend the subject. You said that?"

I nodded again.

"Wyatt Earp. Unbelievable." He shook his head. "I should never have let you keep that .357 Smith & Wesson. What did you call it in the report? Here it is. Model 686. Distinguished combat magnum. I should have made you switch to the semi-auto. The Glock. Plastic. Nothing to say?"

"Nothing to say," I said. Not even raising my head.

"The EMTs were calling it a 'Blue Light Special,' you know, like at Kmart."

I looked over at him.

"Lighten up. That piece of shit deserved it."

"Not my job to decide who deserves it."

"If you didn't sabotage that report I could have kept you on," he said.

"He ended up with 36 stitches," I said.

"If you hadn't waived your right to a pre-deprivation hearing, I could have kept you on."

I just shook my head.

"I put in your retirement papers. I brought your copies," he said.

"Thanks." I nodded.

The Colonel had worked with my father.

* * *

My father loved to drive the family's Plymouth Gran Fury. Four-door hardtop. Inca Gold Metallic. Four hundred and forty horses under the hood.

We'd ride all the way up Route 40 into Wheeling, to the highway marker for McColloch's leap. We would pull off the road at the intersection with Stone Boulevard.

The marker stood just beyond the guardrail overlooking Wheeling Creek. A green patina over the original bronze of the marker, which featured a man astride a horse as it touched the ground on its two front hooves, back legs still in the air. The figure's rifle held one-handed over his head in triumph. The inscription read:

"Major Samuel McCulloch
Daring Scout. Gallant Soldier.
While Attempting the Relief of
Fort Henry at Wheeling
September 1777
Escaped An Overwhelming Body of Indians
By Forcing His Horse Over This Precipice"

"Here," he said. "Stand on the guardrail. Now climb on my shoulders—piggyback." When I did, he neighed like a horse.

150 feet below was Wheeling Creek.

* * *

I was the same age now as my father when he died on the highway during a high-speed chase. A clear night but his radio transmission was garbled. "In pursuit . . . Route 30 . . . suspect vehicle . . ." He never transmitted a description of the suspect vehicle. The Motorola Police Radio Mic still keyed at the time of the crash. Broadcasting. "WHUMP. Crump. Shuushush. CrackleCrinkle. Clink-clink-clink." No one heard the clunk as the microphone dropped from his hand and hit the floorboard. Mic key released. Channel open. His Ford Crown Victoria Police Interceptor was found around a bend against a tree just off the road. It was suicide to drive that fast, 137 miles per hour, around those curves. Killed in the line of duty meant workers comp and insurance benefits for the family. No cancer treatment. No liver transplant. No hospital bills.

A State funeral with all expenses paid.

I wondered what it was like for him at the end. Did the impact obliterate any consciousness of his passing? Did he know he was dead?

My father died being a West Virginia State Trooper.

I decided to die being something else.

* * *

"Anyway," the Colonel said. "That's not really why I'm here. Come take a look." He walked to the back of his Explorer and opened the hatch. A bloodhound was pressed against the rear seat-back. The dog lifted his head, then rested it back on his paws.

"He's not very friendly," I said.

"Disobedient too," the colonel said. "He's not going to work out for us. Too easily distracted. Unfocused. Rambunctious."

The dog stretched, hunched down, and leapt from the back of the vehicle. Stuck his nose in the air. "Sniff . . . Sniffff." Circled. Lay down on the ground. "Huffharumph."

I stared at the dog. He lifted his eyes, then looked back at the ground.

"Couldn't be a show dog either. Not up to the breed standard." Bill knelt by the dog and massaged behind its ears.

"Me neither."

"His head's too big. What?"

"Nothing."

"He's a year old. I didn't want to give him back and I figured you had nothing to do. Something tells me he might be worth keeping. So?"

Belinda, my wife walked out onto the porch, "Hey Bill, what's up?"

"Seein' if Wyatt Earp here wants a dog."

"He's not very friendly," I said.

"Well," she said. "Sometimes the least friendly needs a friend the most." I heard the screen door bang as she walked back inside.

"Is she talking about you or the dog?" Bill asked.

"The dog. I think."

I heard the hinges rasp as the screen door opened and Belinda's voice, doing a Waylon Jennings impression, sang, "Come on, Clyde, we got work to do, that old dog can sing the blues."

The dog lifted its head. Stood up. Ran up to the porch where my wife was waiting by the door. She let Clyde in the house.

"Looks like you got a dog," the colonel said.

* * *

Looking back, that might have been planned. She must have known I would need something to keep me going. That Monday, Doc Black had called in a favor and got us an appointment with a renowned oncologist at Johns Hopkins up in Baltimore.

It was a serious effort. There were three four-week cycles of chemo-therapy. One week of treatment. Three weeks of rest. Repeated three times.

"See you later," was all I could manage whenever I left her.

I was glad I was free of the job. Able to stay home. Take Belinda to her appointments. Be around.

I prayed that I would die first and, in a way where I didn't have to say goodbye.

* * *

On a nice day, during the rest periods between a treatment cycle, we sat under the three white oak trees, just up the rise in the corner of our property. Belinda reclined in her folding aluminum lounge chair. So light now that the crisscrossing white and green nylon straps barely sagged with her in the chair. Suddenly she slapped the wooden handles of the lounge chair, "Bury me here," she said.

Clyde and I startled when her hands clapped the wood. "What? In the yard? Like a dog? Sorry, that was a stupid thing to say," I said.

"Exactly," she said. "And Clyde, when it's his time, here." She pointed at the foot of the lounge chair. Clyde got up and laid down there, panted and grinned. "And you here on my right side." She leaned out of the chair and patted the ground. "Just like the day we walked down the aisle." Then she moved her arms in a circle. "When you file the papers, the county court will give us a 100-foot buffer so that no one can touch the land within that circle." The subject enlivened her. "And don't put dead flowers on my grave. You want me to have flowers, you plant. Perennials, not annuals. The ones that come back every year."

* * *

That night I got up out of bed, dressed in black pants and white shirt. Laced up my old work boots. Still polished, they shined in the moonlight from the window. I buckled on my holster. Grabbed the shovel from the porch and walked out in the yard to dig the grave. I stabbed the ground with the shovel. Again and again, as I paced off three feet and then eight feet. I cut through the grass and into the dirt. A rectangular furrow.

I positioned myself at the edge. I faced east. I heard words: *For as the lightning cometh out of the east, and shineth even unto the west; so shall also the coming of the Son of man be.*

I unholstered my revolver. Placed it in my mouth. As I cocked the hammer with my thumb, the earth gave way behind me. I rolled back on my heels into the pit. Landed on my back face up. The revolver bounced from my hands. As I patted the ground for the revolver, the point of the shovel pressed into my chest and pinned me to the ground. Water rushed in over all four sides at once as if running down a drain. Instantly, I was completely submerged. I reached up with both hands and grabbed the wooden shovel handle. As I did it became a robed arm. The hand curled into a fist that held my shirt and pulled me up. Soaked.

* * *

I awoke sitting up in bed. Belinda was on her side facing me. The dog curled around her feet. I patted my chest and legs in the dark. Dry. Belinda was in her robe, only her feet tucked under the covers. Asleep.

I wondered if you died in your sleep would you know you were dead?

I felt the bed move. The dog crawled up between us and rested his nose on her pillow just below her chin.

* * *

Late that summer, I was sitting at the kitchen table with a bowl of vanilla ice cream reading the *Register-Herald*. Clyde was lying under the table like a rug when all of a sudden he jerked up. Banged his head on the underside of the kitchen table. The spoon rattled from my bowl.

Clyde howled an uncharacteristic, "Roo. Ro-Rooo."

His nails clattered across the linoleum floor and down the hall.

The screen door was latched. Clyde leapt. I heard the screen rip and the door panel clatter onto the porch.

When I got to the porch, Clyde was already across the road and behind the windbreak of trees. I heard him splash into the pond. I watched for him from the porch. He trotted back through the trees, trailing water and carrying an old canvas mail sack in his mouth. He stepped back through the door with the sack still in his mouth. He set it on the floor of the kitchen. He shook off the water, then bent and chewed the rope apart. He poked his snout inside and one at a time lifted out three kittens. All were grey tabbies striped with white underbellies. One of them was dead. Its head smashed. Two of them began to meow. I looked inside the sack. Nothing else but a large flat rock.

Belinda walked up the stairs from the cellar. Shifted the laundry basket on her hip. The clothes inside were neatly folded. "What's all the commotion?" She said.

"Mister. Hey Mister."

I walked to the front porch.

"Your dog took my sack," the boy said from the other side of the road.

I marched down toward him and he took off at a run. I caught him just by the edge of the trees. Picked him up by his belt and his collar and carried him out into the pond.

"Mister. Hey. Mister! I can't swim. I can't swim!" he said.

I wasn't listening. I lifted him over my head and threw him into the middle of the pond and walked back to the house.

I didn't see Clyde. Belinda stood at the door. She held the laundry basket out in front of her. Two kittens peaked out from under a folded towel. "You never could abide cruelty. But cruelty is no way to teach that boy not to be cruel."

I turned around and walked back out onto the porch. The boy was sitting next to Clyde near the edge of the pond. Both dripped water. A swath of the dirt turned to mud where Clyde had dragged the boy up on the shore.

"Clyde's got him," I said to her over my shoulder.

* * *

We got the latest test results the next day. Remission. The cancer was gone. She had beaten it back. The cancer had retreated. For now.

I was afraid it was only hiding. But I got tired of being old and feeling like waiting was all that was left.

"No more moping," she said. "Find something to do."

* * *

I called Owen Landon. We had worked together from time to time while I was a state trooper. Owen was tall and lean. He had been a state champion hurdler in high school and still looked it.

He had trained bloodhounds for law enforcement agencies across the country for over 25 years and was a member of the Barbour County Tactical Search and Recovery Teams in West Virginia. He invited us up to his home in Philippi to evaluate Clyde.

Owen said, "Clyde descended from the oldest hounds that hunt by scent still in existence."

He then quoted from the 235AD treatise, *Historia Animalium*, by the Roman Scholar Aelian. ". . . of a hound with, unrivaled scenting powers, so intensely devoted to his work that he could not be pulled off the trail until his quarry was found."

Owen continued, "The name bloodhound does not refer to any blood tracking ability, but in medieval times in Western Europe monks bred hounds for the bishops who liked to 'ride to hounds,' as they hunted." These hounds were bred on the grounds of the monasteries. Their breeding was so carefully conducted by the monks that their hounds came to be known as "blooded hounds." Meaning "of aristocratic blood."

"Not," Owen repeated, "because of any blood tracking ability."

A bloodhound is designed for tracking.

The loose, wrinkled skin around his face traps scent particles. The drooping ears sweep odors from the ground into his nostrils as he walks.

His long neck, muscular shoulders, and strong back, enable him to keep his nose to the ground for miles on end.

Clyde padded around the living room sniffing and poking his head under the couch pillows as Owen, 'The Professor of Bloodhound-ology' explained, "A bloodhound has a large set of ultrasensitive scent membranes that enables it to distinguish smells at least a thousand times better than humans. No man-made scenting device is as accurate as a bloodhound's nose."

I nodded.

"You got a dime? Find a dime. Hold it out."

I did.

"OK. That is your—a human being's—olfactory center." He stepped into the kitchen. Clattered around a bit. Held out a Thanksgiving dinner serving platter through the doorway. "That's Clyde's."

The dog walked over and sniffed the platter.

"That won't fit in his head."

Owen side armed the platter at me like a Frisbee. It bounced harmlessly on the couch. "You're going to be harder to train than the dog."

Owen never seems to be joking.

Owen wanted to train Clyde as an air-scenting search dog. As such, Clyde would not be restricted to searching for a missing person's track but would be able to search even after the track had been obliterated.

"When a bloodhound sniffs a scent article—any item touched ONLY by the subject—the sniffs rush air through his nasal cavity and the odors lodge in the mucus and bombard the dog's scent receptors. Chemical signals travel to the olfactory bulb, that's the part of the brain that analyzes smells . . ."

"The dinner platter," I said.

"And an 'odor image' is created," he said as he rolled his eyes.

"For the dog, this image is far more detailed than a photograph is for you and me. Using the odor image as a reference, the bloodhound can locate a subject's trail."

"Once the bloodhound identifies the trail, it will not divert its attention despite being assailed by a multitude of other odors."

"A bloodhound must be relentless in his tasks," Owen said. "So, I know what a bloodhound can do. I need to know what you can do."

* * *

He ran us through an obstacle course with ramps, seesaws, tables, and tunnels. Clyde pulled me through most of it but balked at the tunnel. A little coaxing got him through. As I ran around the tunnel to the other side Owen pointed at me. "Back through same as the dog."

"Sheesh."

"While I work with the dog for a bit. Why don't you go for a run."

"A run?"

"You're going to have to be able to stay with the dog as much as you can. Or catch up to him. Clyde needs to train, so do you."

"A run? Where?"

"Just around here. Through the woods. Like a steeplechase—up and over—around and through. Cross country style."

I started out into the woods.

"I'll whistle for you when it's time to head back."

Looking down at my feet, I shook my head and started jogging.

"That trail goes for about two miles, so down and back."

When I returned, Owen and Clyde were waiting on the porch. I almost slurped water right out of the dog bowl, but Owen handed me a YETI 18-ounce water bottle engraved with a K9 search and rescue with paw cross emblem. Wrapped around the bottom of the bottle was a piece of beige masking tape with "In Training" written in Sharpie.

Maybe people get lost so others can find their way.

* * *

During training, Owen outfitted Clyde with a blaze orange protective vest that strapped on his back and protected his belly. A GPS tracker collar and a copper cowbell went around his neck. "This way I could hear him, you could hear him, and so could whomever he was searching for," Owen said. "And we don't need to follow some damn beeping that sounds like a backin-up truck."

"The dog pursues the lost. You pursue the dog," he said as he waved Clyde and me away.

We trained for almost two years.

Owen sponsored us in the mock exercises organized by the Appalachian Search and Rescue Conference and MARG, the Mountain Area Rescue Group.

There would be three mock exercises that year, spring, summer, and fall.

Belinda wished us well as we headed off for each exercise. Always with the same final words for me. *Nothing better happen to that dog.*

The spring exercise was held at Coopers Rock State Forest. It was Clyde's cold trail test. A bloodhound has the capability to follow tracks over 300 hours old. Our lost subject hiked the 2.5-mile Raven Rock trail 120 hours (5 days) before we arrived at the park and was hidden (camped) behind a big boulder near the overlook at the end of the trail.

As an air-scenting dog, Clyde was trained to work off-lead and follow a diffused scent working perpendicular to the wind. A typical search for Clyde would be about 40–160 acres. He would be able to detect the source of a scent up to a quarter mile away.

All humans, alive or dead, constantly emit microscopic particles bearing human scent made up of skin cells, hygiene products, bacteria, fungus, sweat, hormones, and enzymes. Millions of these mini cornflake-like bits are airborne and are carried by the wind for considerable distances. These skin rafts are what Clyde would be tracking. His paws would be on the ground but the trail he followed would be in the air.

It was a rocky trail that slopes downward, flattens, and ends with a steep incline with no railings. It was posted with warnings. A misstep could lead to a potentially fatal fall. But there were no missteps. Clyde navigated his way flawlessly to the lost hiker.

Owen told us as we left the park that it got its name from a legend about an outlaw that hid near the overlook. He was a cooper by trade and continued to make barrels at his new hideout.

"He wouldn't have been able to hide from Clyde," I told him.

"Hide from Clyde." Owen shook his head.

The summer exercise was held in the Monongahela National Forest. Monongahela because the forest was located in the watershed from that river. The river was named by the original people who lived here, the Lenape. In their language it was spelled MENAWNGIHELLA, and translated meant falling banks because the river's banks often caved into the water.

Belinda came with us on this training exercise. It was one of her favorite places.

It reminded her of her father.

"Now look over here," her father had told her. "This is our state tree. We call it the sugar maple or rock maple. You know what makes it so special?"

"Syrup," she said as she walked over and picked up a leaf from the ground.

"True, but there's something else. It is the most shade tolerant of all the large hardwood trees. Unusual for this big of a tree. Shade tolerant means—it can grow in the shade while it waits for the sun. And then when the other trees let the sunlight in," he picked her up and swung her in a circle and set her down in a patch of sunlight between the trees. "Our tree here grows as fast as it can to reach up to the sky."

She laughed and jumped up with her hand into the sunlight as far as she could.

She always remembered that day in the woods. Her first hike in the Monongahela National Forest. The rock maple. The sun and her father.

She pointed out the state trees as we came across them but neither Clyde nor I could decipher one from the rest.

At the Lindy Point Overlook above Blackwater Canyon, she told Clyde, and me, the story of the forest.

* * *

"By 1914 all the trees had been clear-cut from this canyon. Not one tree standing from here all the way to the river. As if the forest had been shaved away from the face of the earth," she said. "The logging left behind stumps, slashings, twigs, and residual sawdust."

I looked down into the canyon. *A tinderbox,* I thought.

"The fire burned for six months. It left no remnants of any tree at all. Only thin mineral soil and base rock. But one hundred years later, all these trees have come back. A second growth." She smiled.

Beautiful.

Clyde would be tested for only 60 miles in the Blackwater Canyon of the forest. The scent trail was made by an ATV dragging a pack of 'smelly' clothes for thirty miles through the canyon. It was Clyde's endurance test.

A determined bloodhound can stick to a trail for 130 miles.

The scent article is the cover of a jigsaw puzzle box. The bloodhound searches ground and air for pieces that fit to make the picture. When enough lock together the search is on.

Clyde can run an average of 19 miles per hour.

It was a timed trial. We finished late. The steel-pipe gate across the access road was locked. The backpack was just up the hill.

The judge smiled at Clyde. "Sorry, Big Guy, time's up."

Clyde panting. Me bent over, hands on my knees. Panting.

Then Clyde ran back and forth along the gate. Midway he leapt almost straight up, flopped, like Dick Fosbury doing the high jump at the 1968 Summer Olympics, cleared the gate and landed onto his shoulder. Rolled and was up. The cowbell on his collar clink clanked as he ran.

I stepped on the bottom pipe, sidesaddled the top, swung my legs over and dropped. I ran after Clyde.

Clyde sat behind the evaluator's car. The backpack was in the trunk.

The fall test was at Hawks Nest State Park. It was Clyde's distraction test. The test was held during the Country Roads Festival in September. Lots of distractions. Clyde got diverted twice. Once to the nine-hole golf course and again at Mill Creek. Not a good day. He should have found the 'lost child' at the beginning of Lover's Leap trail but didn't before the test ended.

"More practice," Owen said.

* * *

The Summers County Sheriff turned into the parking lot in his cruiser. I got out to shake hands and he gave me a rundown from yesterday.

The boy had just come back with his mother and baby sister from the John Henry Days Festival in Talcott.

John Henry Days was an annual three-day festival held on the second weekend of July. The festival starts on Friday night with a concert at the stage near the Great Bend Tunnel and ends on Sunday with the Rubber Duck Race at the Talcott Bridge overlooking the Greenbrier River.

The sheriff showed me yesterday's picture of the boy.

There was a statute of John Henry that commemorated his 1870 contest with the steam drill near the entrance to the Great Bend Tunnel of the C & C Railroad in John Henry Historical Park.

It is believed that John Henry was killed by a faulty explosion or rock fall during the construction of the Great Bend Tunnel. He was buried, along with the other railroad workers killed during the building of the tunnel, in an unmarked grave just outside the tunnel entrance, under the statue of John Henry, right where the little boy posed for the picture.

In the picture, the boy stood in front of the brick pedestal that held the eight-foot bronze statue of a standing John Henry. The figure of a man was shirtless, the metal black as coal. A long sledgehammer was held across his body. John Henry, ready to draw that hammer back over his shoulder for another swing. The boy in his WVU t-shirt, a determined grimace on his face, held his plastic toy hammer just like John Henry in the statue. The boy's head was even with John Henry's left boot, the toy hammer held just above the final words on the bronze plaque.

> ". . . John Henry died in a race with a steam drill, during construction of the tunnel for the C & O Railroad Company. May God grant that we always respect the great and the strong and be of service to others . . ."

The Sheriff said, "Follow me. I'll bring you over to meet Leanna and get started."

As we followed the sheriff, I couldn't help thinking of the ballad.

"I'd die with a hammer in my hand, Lord, Lord,
I'd die with a hammer in my hand."

Before we left, I had asked the Sheriff why he called me and he said, "The mother, she asked for you. Well, she asked for the dog, because of his picture in the newspaper."

"That was a fluke," I said.

"That's what you say," the sheriff said and started his cruiser. He called out the window, "But what's the dog say?"

That winter after the failure at Hawks Nest, Owen called us to practice at an ongoing winter search in Wood County where a teenager had gone missing. At the end of the day, Clyde ended up sitting out on frozen Woodmount Lake. When the Sheriff ended the search for the day, I called Clyde back to the car, but he wouldn't come. He stood then sat back down in the same place.

A Parkersburg reporter from the *News & Sentinel* snapped the picture.

I called Clyde again. Clyde, his paws slipping, walked over to the Subaru and we left.

That spring the lake had thawed and a fisherman came across the teenager's body near the shore. The article in the paper when the teenager was found ran the picture of Clyde with the caption, "Resolute." In the picture, Clyde sat, orange vest bright against the white of the frozen lake, a glint off the cooper cowbell in the sun, one ear blown behind his head and the other flapped out from the side like a flag.

There was also a picture of the boy as he looked before he went missing.

I parked out front in the midst of the other vehicles. Clyde sat in the passenger seat as I buckled on his vest, turned on the GPS, snapped it around his neck, and clipped the cowbell to his collar.

A crowd of people watched as I opened the door for Clyde. A woman passed through the small crowd holding a hamper full of the boy's dirty clothes. She set it down in front of Clyde, like an offering, and backed away. He looked at me. I nodded. His head disappeared in the hamper of clothes. The pile of clothes bumped up and down as he snuffed around. He backed up and sat at my feet. Still.

"Search."

Clyde lifted his head in the air. He shook his head as his big ears flapped and sat still again. Then he breathed, deep breaths through his nose. In, out, one, two. Like a bellows looking for a spark. Clyde stood, crouched, and then he was off. The cowbell clanged in rhythm with the big dog's pace as he ran.

Yesterday's search had been in the wrong direction.

When Jeremy left the house, he carried his toy hammer and the engine from his train set. He caught the back door with his foot as it closed, so it wouldn't slam, and eased it shut. He did not head toward the dry creek bed where he usually played but instead walked around front and down the road awhile before he crossed over into the trees.

He hammered the ground and the trees to clear the way for his railway. He ran from time to time slaloming the trees. "Chugachuga chuga chuga whoo whoo," he hollered over and over again.

The light faded.

He ran his toy engine along the trunk of an uprooted sycamore tree. He sat down at the end and leaned against the tangled dirt and branches of the root ball. The tree that had toppled was so big that he had to stand on tiptoes to look over the top of the root ball. He looked back for the way he came. But he couldn't see it. He was lost.

The sun began to set. He was tired. Worried. He remembered what his mother told him at the festival yesterday. *If you get lost. If we get separated. Stay put. Don't keep wandering around. Stay put. I will find you.*

Jeremy nodded to himself and sat down against the tree.

He dozed. Startled. He woke. He looked out into the dusk. He thought he saw a dog in between the trees facing him. It had reddish and grey fur and its ears peaked upward. The eyes shone yellow. It was not a dog. It was a fifty-pound coyote that stood two feet at the shoulder and was five feet long from its nose to the tip of its tail.

Jeremy threw his hammer. It rattled off a tree. Then his toy train, but it fell short of the coyote. Jeremy scrambled around for a clod of dirt. He threw it. Not far enough. "Go away." He grabbed another clod of dirt and stood up. The coyote moved toward him. Jeremy threw that clod, missed the coyote, and hit a tree. The coyote sidestepped the spray of dirt and moved closer. Jeremy picked up a branch and jabbed it in the direction of the coyote. He scraped the ground in an arc in front of him, windshield-wiped the dirt. The coyote backed away and wandered off.

Jeremy was cold. He tried to stay awake but couldn't. He dozed until a rustling woke him.

The coyote pounced. It huffed and chomped as it ate the rabbit.

Jeremy could not tell where the sound came from. He glanced all around as the sunlight rose into the forest.

The coyote was back to where it had been before. It watched the boy. Sniffed and stepped forward with its head down. It growled as Jeremy picked up the branch.

Jeremy heard a clang clang from behind him, a bark, and then a deep rumble of a growl. A big dog in an orange vest appeared beside Jeremy, on his right.

Tired, confused, Jeremy thought at first it was McGruff, The Crime Dog that had been at the last day of school before summer and warned of "Stranger Danger." Jeremy glanced again. He was afraid to take his eyes from the coyote for more than an instant. It was a real dog. The big bloodhound was three inches taller at the shoulder and twice as heavy as the coyote. It moved in front of Jeremy.

But the bloodhound had never been hungry or hunted food. The bloodhound had never fought and never killed.

Searching was trained. Protecting was instinct.

The bloodhound charged. Divots of dirt splattered Jeremy. The coyote leapt away but stopped when the bloodhound did. The coyote snarled. Lips pulled back. Teeth bared.

Jeremy cringed from the snarling. Held his knees close to his chest. Tucked in his chin.

The coyote leapt. The bloodhound reared up on its hind legs. They collided. Wrestled on their hind legs. The coyote's jaws snapped at the bloodhound's throat but closed on the cowbell instead. The bloodhound twisted its big head. It bludgeoned the coyote. Knocked it down to the ground on its side. The coyote scrambled to its feet. Juked away. The bloodhound's jaws snapped on the air. The bloodhound fronted the coyote. Blocked its path to the boy.

I ran around the fallen tree. I saw Clyde. I saw the coyote. I didn't see the boy. I threw the handheld GPS receiver at the coyote but missed. The coyote flinched. I lunged at the coyote as if to tackle it but tripped over an exposed tree root and fell flat on my chest.

'Blam!' I covered my ears. 'Blamblamblam!' The sheriff knelt beside me. 'Blam! Blam! Click.' The big revolver smoked over my head.

"Nice shooting," I said.

"I missed," he said. We watched the coyote run off.

"Oh. I thought you were aiming at the tree."

He patted me on the back and stood up.

I looked over my shoulder. Clyde sat next to the boy who huddled against him for warmth. Blood dripped from Clyde's torn ear.

Belinda's going to kill me when she sees that.

As I got to my feet, Jeremy's mother ran from around the tree and hugged him to the ground, crying.

"I knew you'd find me," Jeremy said to her.

Sent Away

The crescent sweep of conifer-furred mountains
against clay sky, the river's scouring rush

past twisted roots, and seven years
separated me from blood-stained grout,

my mother's hand
ending in a razor, her will

to kill us both
as I slept in her womb, the promise

of the pillow my father pressed
over my sister's face. Facts

I couldn't know, but I knew
the black wing of death in the chattering catalpa

and swollen gray children
on the bottom of the iced-over pond.

In my bones, I shared
their cold marrow. Questions

shuddered like the hawk's shadow on tall grass.
Under the half-hearted mountain laurel,

in a bed of horse chestnut roots
and dank leaves, the earth opened,

unctuous and inviting, where I waited,
crushing the waxy yellow meat

of buckeyes, their rotting scent
on me that wouldn't wash off.

Square Knots

My son and I practice tying knots. He seeks
a merit badge. I was a Scout, and on my honor
I've made many promises to God, to country,
to people tied to me. I've been tying knots all my life.

Only now can I say precisely the steps to make a
square knot—or reef knot—every time and not
the unstable granny. A square knot requires rope ends
parallel to the rope's standing part to avoid slippage.

Sailors use square knots to reef sails to cross spars.
My life has been trial and error, but I chant the formula
as my son crosses over two whipped ends of rope:
"Right over left and under. Left over right and under."

Your belly knots up in these moments of clarity, and
you desire to go back to recover severed lines, the
opportunities, the devastation you've made of
relationships, the bitterness, the scenes in public.

You haul in and tie down what you can, live
with the lanyards flapping in air, ripped sails,
dull lashes from a storm-torn past. I wish for him
merit badges and a life not haunted by loose ends.

On the Porch

What I called *tragedy* you labeled
     disappointment, for you had the grander
perspective, knew nothing terrible
     would come from a heart broken by the likes
of that. The real question was how we'd
     ever come together in the first place,
the answer what I really needed
     to mourn, the self with sense, who knew things
before others, the eyes that saw mistakes
     way in advance. While I talked, you sat in
a chair and watched the valley slowly
     come to you, beginning with the clouds like
flat-bottomed puffs arriving in lines
     one after the other like guardian
angels there to testify about
     what is approaching behind them, theirs the
first wave, the one that signals and warns
     though the sun is shining, the wind still mild.

A Muggy Spring Night

A hide-and-seek moon,
community center's closed.
The boys are on their own.

At the edge of town,
sons gather in the shadow
of the World War II hero,
pool money for gas and beer,
rev engines, cruise the square.
Every boy slipping into
the rut left behind
by his old man's tire tracks.

Steeped in warm beer,
sweat and hormones,
boys hoot and holler,
wave sloshing bottles at passersby,
hang from car windows,
jerked back from the maw of blacktop
and cinders.
Boys, high on gas fumes,
burning rubber,
cheap beer and
girls, girls, girls,
slow, shout pickup lines—

"That the best you can do, Joe?
Ain't no girl gonna fall for that!"
But a few do.

Girls squeeze in breast to shoulder,
thigh rubbing thigh,
drinking and flirting.
They glance through the fogged windows,
search for a bold neon arrow
pointing the way
to Somewhere Else.
The car too slow,
the night a blur.
Untested hearts racing
with insatiable desire
to bury their unfamiliar ache
beneath oil-slicked asphalt,
sex and beer.

Box Seat Video Cresson, PA

Friday night payday flyers
looking to annihilate the week
moms shepherding kids
in little league uniforms
into minivans
buzz over the busted pavement
my rust-laden Buick Century
mingles in the parking lot
with pickups with missing tailgates

State Store   Box Seat Video   beer distro
the promise of pepperoni pizza to go
around the corner
this might as well be
the crossroads of the known world

I'm here for
Aftershock   Pabst
and a piece
of Hollywood on VHS
for when the lights go down
in the living rooms of Cambria County

We're all here to break
the boredom of watching
the shrinking possibilities
of small-town days
a slight warm and fuzzy feel
a movie just boring enough
there's no need to pause the tape
before couch sex
and our little promise of heaven

Rania Zuri

Musings of an Appalachian Winter

No more leaves
The apple butter cools
Mee-Maw hollers over yonder, as the sun sets
The family groundhog nowhere to be seen
The pepperoni roll still warm in my mind, but so cold in my hands
I brace myself for a brutal winter
The harsh snow blocking me in
I sigh and start making molasses
What else is there to do?
Hillbilly is what people call me
But I am not an Appalachian stereotype . . . or so I tell myself
I look down at my pepperoni roll now cold, unappetizing
Just another Appalachian winter comes and goes
The maple syrup thaws, thawing my heart
Sweet as sugar is once more
Pour it in my grits
The energy I didn't know I needed
To survive another Appalachian winter

A Dead-End Road to Home

Swaths of black-eyed Susan, Queen Anne's lace, and clover fall as my dog and I set out on our morning walk. The county has sent a crew of one to mow the ditch line of our one-lane road. The driver himself is harmless enough, considerate even, stopping to let us pass safely by. He is only doing his job, and yet, I want to ask him to please stop. I get that many see these plants as weeds. I understand that they harbor at least four species of disease-ridden ticks. I've also seen how this profusion of greenery and blossoms shelters everything from turtles to rabbits, how it feeds birds and butterflies. What's the harm in leaving things as they are? This road doesn't go anywhere, after all. That is, it doesn't go anywhere in a literal sense. In my heart, it takes me hundreds of miles and half a life away from here in Kentucky to the Finger Lakes and Southern Tier, places where I grew up and that much of my family still call home. As for me, I've spent twenty years trying to claim this new-to-me corner of Appalachia as my own. I still don't know if it has claimed me in return. I could spend a lifetime learning what it needs, which parts can be tamed, and which should be left unruly and wild. Human connections, on the other hand, are another story. Even though I come from a place not unlike this one, I keep encountering a gap that seems impossible to cross. Sometimes, it's a matter of geography — Appalachia, some were taught, ends in Ohio. Other times, it's the apparent paradox of Appalachia and New York. I don't even pronounce the former correctly, after all, while the latter is populated by a bunch of city-dwelling snobs. How can someone like me say she belongs in this mountain place?

I know a preteen girl who could explain it well, if people would give her half a chance. I remember her at 10 or 11, walking along a different dead-end road, outside a town with a single stoplight. Her blond hair is contained in a sloppy approximation of a French braid (she doesn't have the patience to learn to do it right). She doesn't yet need glasses, but she's on year two of the endless orthodontia that never will make her teeth quite straight. She is wearing her favorite tee-shirt, a souvenir from a camping trip, along with well-worn jeans. It's not that she minds getting dressed up; she even enjoys it from time to time. It's just that today, as most days, she's thinking about other things.

She wanders up the lane, chewing a stalk of timothy as she picks some stems of Daisy, then Black-eyed Susan and Queen Anne's Lace. She pauses before the blue Chicory, wondering why it gets dismissed, along with the Queen Anne's Lace, as little more than a weed. She tries to pick some, but the tough stems dissuade her. It won't be part of her country girl's bouquet. She knows she should head back to the trailer, save her grandmother the trouble of calling her in for supper. She just needs to recover a little more first. The drive from the northern end of Keuka Lake might not be long, but the twisting, plunging Steuben County roads always make her carsick, especially when she rides in the way-back seat. Until the queasiness eases, her grandparents' living room will feel too small, the TV too large, the conversation uncomfortably loud. The expanse of sun and sky, the uncultivated fields, these provide the remedy she seeks.

What would that girl have said if someone had told her that four decades later, she would choose to make her home just one mile from another plunging, twisting mountain road? Perhaps she would not have believed it. Then again, maybe she already knew that the things she loved then would always matter, despite or maybe because of the wild and winding roads it takes to find them.

She watches with me this warm June morning as the mower turns around, continuing its implacable path toward town. We both know these plants will grow back, just as they always have, in Kentucky as in New York. With them will come the mulleins, ironweed, and touch-me-nots, referred to here as jewelweed—a name that I would have found as delightful at age 11 as I do now at 51. Our dead-end road is limitless, opulent with fresh growth and the promise of home.

Under the Velvet Elvis

It's carried over the 50,000-watt
Beacon of six o'clock Mine Reports whose dark
Doxologies call to who will and who won't work—
Before the power goes down a second time.

Prayers and candles gig across a wall
Slick with mirrors. The floor's meticulously
Swept plywood whispers like a devotee,
As a nylon smock twisted becomes a swan,

Resting on a swivel back, third chair down.
But in repose, deeper, the owner's son
Reclined, head back, at the hair washing station
Hasn't moved at all. He's been there for weeks.

Having draped him in flowers, lit the incense,
Mother and Aunt, who brought him to this office,
Claim a honey sweet scent, or a black licorice,
Or the vapor of twice baked bread will rise

Over his cheekbones taut as an oil drum.
His curls drift, rigid, in the flickering bath,
The petals beside him floating. There is a faith
Arrived at when any steel mill shuts its doors,

Or a mine closes, with only a sign and a chain
To hold the wageless back from their guerdons:
Sacrifice binds us to the chorus. Unions
Bargain as the young lie back in their living graves.

And so the sisters keep an empty business,
Watch over the register that will be opened,
Wash his hair with ginseng, their charge attend,
His waxen lip worked nightly, rockabilly.

Below the brushed images of The King
Sounds of a hundred country stations revel
For all the young ones (all their dreams fulfill),
Hushed as sleeping Adams. The static jumps.

One can almost make out guitar, a man
Of conviction; the other, who he would
Have married had the economy allowed.
Hear them singing what he could have been.

Willie Nelson's Back in Town

for my brother

Somehow
it has carried this far: across fifty miles
and more than forty years; the strains of a song,
acres rippling with people, the rising sun.

We slept with the hatchback open; Baby Brother's
six-foot-six self sticking out, people knew who
he was, just from those legs
at Legend Valley
when Willie Nelson led a Dixie Jam.

Coffee-colored curls
bobbed above the crowd, trees throbbed
with the echoes of bass. It was all glory then;
rain and mud were nothing to us.

We reached for the stars
in a clearing by the woods,
before the world separated and the road
led to other seasons, into trembling darkness, into
humiliations and regrets. Back then we rose up on tiptoes,
shook out our hair, screamed with delight.

In memory
the safe places never change.
How otherwise could I have come to this, clarified,
leaning one way and then another,
humming a favorite old tune.

We Need to Talk About Ohio

There's something about punk from the Midwest
maybe it's the finality of all that land
being so far from the ocean
no possibility for primordial escape back
into the water leads
to casual aesthetic madness
except Cleveland's got the lake
and they're the craziest motherfuckers of all
setting off fireworks in a basement with only one exit
Electric Eels running over guitar cables
with a lawnmower, kicking cops in the nuts
that landscaper themed hardcore band
with the leaf blowers full of gold confetti
Uncle Bob is drinking in Dayton
a hundred albums in and he's still
singing improvised surrealist lyrics like a hymn
he's known his whole life
bands like Vacation and Brainiac
that you've probably never heard of
but you probably should
and like EdfromOhio they're starting to move here
Totally Miguel and Jimmy Rose
invading our wooded hills
most greet them as liberators
the Ohio weird is sinking in
taking over Pittsburgh
and I don't know if
I want to be saved

Honey

Our backs on an October-cold parking lot
in the dark of Nowhere, West Virginia, we watch

silvery shooting stars that make
us catch our breath.

A patient died today. His face—
greasy white translucence, eyes

rolled back—before me,
so you bring me here

where I can feel your body's
familiar warmth, hand cupping mine.

Motionless on tarmac—we float
in space, plan to buy land, plant

exotic clovers, raise bees
for honey. Because you like

the algorithms of their genes,
slowness coaxed with smoke,

I want you content, our love
the centerpiece in miles of green humming.

Unable to take our eyes from the ribbons
of light, we shiver. The dead

patient must have done this: studied
the stars, planned, lain beside his wife, sweetened

so by death that pain and joy
became inseparable, one from the other.

Monday Morning

I'd barely had time to sit down, dump my purse and keys into the dented bottom drawer of the metal desk, and nudge it closed with my knee before my first visitors showed up. Monday mornings normally bring clients trickling in wanting Band-Aids or aspirin. Some just want to push back on the start of the work week, chew the fat, chit-chat about the weekend—sometimes theirs, but more often than not, mine. They're a nebby bunch. Today's visitors didn't hold much with tradition, but then, this wasn't looking to be a typical Monday.

Without knocking, a posse of my colleagues filed into the tiny clinic where I serve the workers and clients of the sheltered workshop. Mumbling into Styrofoam cups and huddling together tight as a flock of sheep on market day, they waited uncomfortably for someone to take the lead. Their anxiety started to rub off on me; my skin began to prickle. I wondered what I'd done now and if I'd worked long enough to collect unemployment.

My stomach sank when Mr. Hahn, our supervisor, walked in. He's a backward, fair-to-middling manager even on his best days. His preferred mode of correspondence with staffers is rambling memos on lined, yellow paper stuffed into workroom pigeonholes. To soften bad news, he sometimes adds a personal touch by way of his secretary; Jenny will hand a note directly to you or leave it face up on your desk if you're away.

So, imagine my surprise when Mr. Hahn stepped forward, adjusted his stained tie, cleared his throat, and began his recitation. I did my best to listen respectfully as Mr. Hahn rambled on, repeating several times his need to inform me about something that had apparently happened over the weekend, something that everyone else in the room already knew. I was starting to feel a little put off by the focus on me until finally, it sank in that he was talking about our client, Anna. Suddenly, I felt as though I was being swept away in a flash flood, drawn into foamy brown water—the kind that stinks of earthworms and regret and washes one yelling and thrashing down a sewer drain with all your unresolved junk sucked in with you.

From that point on, Mr. Hahn's story rushed by in a torrent of facts and irrelevant comments, most of which flowed like muddy debris into one ear and out the other, all but the knowledge of what had become of Anna—that had been forever seared onto my brain.

Mr. Hahn, anxious as ever to pass the buck, ended his speech with, "We've decided *you* should be the one to go. After all, *you're* the nurse."

Jenny gave him an incredulous look and turned to me, "We're so sorry, Hon. We'll be here for you when you get back."

The remaining staff, all my elders by at least a couple of decades, stood quietly with eyes downcast or gazed at fly specks on the clinic's dingy window to avoid looking me in the eye.

Stunned, I only nodded and then watched as my coworkers jostled one another in their hurry to get out the door behind Mr. Hahn. Lemmings came to mind until I got to thinking that we weren't playing follow the leader. I alone was being shoved over the cliff. Gripping the edge of my battered desk, I steadied myself and held back threatening tears. I dared not allow myself their pleasure. Not yet.

Me, all of twenty-one, fresh out of nursing school, a starched and folded nurse's cap bobby-pinned on my head, found myself sitting there thinking about what I had been taught. The nuns saw to it that our training covered more than how to fold square corners on a hospital bed, take temps, pass meds and kiss doctors' butts. The sisters' focus was teaching duty and responsibility as a divine calling. I think the celestial line may have rung busy when The Divine tried my number. Still, I knew my duty was to my client and friend, Anna.

* * *

Anna was a frequent visitor to my little clinic; she wasn't much younger than me—could have been my little sister. On good days she heard voices muffled in soggy, gray clouds; on others, her thoughts might rattle with thunder as lightning illuminated all sorts of perceived dangers.

She lived exposed, unprotected. She had learned to get by on smarts, humor, and pill-induced numbness.

Though Anna was on my Wednesday therapy schedule, she finagled her way into my clinic most weekdays by surprising me with ailments pulled from my old nursing books, but headaches remained her favorite. There was so much you could do with a headache, like milk it until it mutated into a migraine. Anna's treatment of choice was lounging away an afternoon on the clinic cot listening to my radio, avoiding her job in the workshop while remaining on the clock and collecting her pay. I enjoyed her company, and sometimes we even touched upon the issues that she smothered with silliness. We both knew what our time together was actually billed as, but it was never mentioned. Anna treated 'therapy' like a four-letter word. She'd catch me in the hall with, "Hey! We're still getting together Wednesday afternoon at one, right?" I'd nod yes as she rushed by on her way to the break room.

This past Friday I was sitting at my desk counting down the fifteen minutes until I could lock up and leave. I heard hesitant footsteps in the hallway come to a halt outside the clinic. Anna stuck her head through the door and dramatically whispered, "Goodbye." She cuddled the doorframe and leaned in, "I'm going home for the weekend. Daddy's picking me up in the morning." She hesitated before adding, "I can't say no."

I let her words swirl around the ceiling fan a few seconds too long, giving me time to think up an answer. I knew she'd never liked the long rides home with her father. In the past, when I'd brought up their relationship, she'd clam up. This time it was me playing dumb, ignoring her hints that silently shouted, "I need to talk." I was anxious to finish my paperwork and grab my paycheck from Jenny on the way out. I had dinner plans.

"See you Monday!" I replied brightly, fluttering my fingers in an abbreviated wave. "You'll have fun! It's been months since you've been home; you're ready as you'll ever be. Tell your mom 'Hi' for me. Oh, and if she wants to send you back with some of her snickerdoodles, tell her I said they won't go to waste!"

I bent to sign my time sheet. I let my hair fall across my face to block Anna out. I didn't glance up again until only the echoes of her footsteps loitered outside my door. Guilt was already getting comfy in the pit of my stomach. As an excuse, I told myself I'd have more time to spend with her come Monday morning.

The short string that connected Friday to today had stretched to the length of a lifetime. Yes, I'd go; Anna would want me to be the one. I hung the be-back-soon sign on the clinic door and set the red plastic hands on the foolish, little clock face ahead by one hour. Then, I bullied my reluctant feet until they gave in and carried me to my car out in the parking lot.

* * *

I found the funeral director in his office. I must have been expected; no doubt Jenny had called ahead. One glance at my uniform and he apparently felt no need to waste perfunctory pleasantries or condolences on me; he knew that I was on the clock. My greeting and outstretched hand were ignored. His priggish body language made it clear that he was anxious to be done with me. I hoped that he was more polite to the dead.

His introduction was nothing more than a snippet, "Miss Carter? Abel Harrington." He grabbed a key ring from his desk and jangled it with authority. He headed through his office door calling, "Let's go," his voice a curt demand.

He motioned for me to follow. I was fine with the scant conversation; it made it easier to hold myself together. I'd crumble if he chose to offer even fake kindness.

I didn't question him as he led me out the back door of the main building to the parking lot. Once outside, I exhaled the stale air of the funeral parlor. Maybe Mr. Hahn was wrong and I wasn't needed after all. Someone else had stepped up. Surely Mr. Harrington was going to thank me for my trouble and direct me to my car.

No. Mr. Harrington continued across the driveway to a garage. I half ran to keep up, my sensible, white shoes slowing me down as I watched him from behind; a nervous laugh that refused to be squelched crept up my throat. His gait and severe black suit brought to mind an actor playing an undertaker in an old spaghetti western. Mortified, I paused and bent over, covering my mouth and turning away, hoping to disguise my ill-timed giggle as a coughing fit. He turned and glared as if he'd read my mind.

"Allergies," I mumbled and waved apologetically toward the flowering crabapple trees dotting the manicured lawn. The trees were lovely, maintaining a solemn dignity befitting their station. Still, I felt for those trees. Anyone who'd take the time to look could see they longed to pack up their trunks and transplant themselves to a place where they could blow their petals like kisses to folks passing by, not drop them like tears.

We stopped at the garage. My host turned to me with a smirk, unlocked the overhead door and forced it up. Darkness rolled out from beneath the door and the sunlight shrank back and refused to enter the musty, dank interior. The door jammed halfway up, but Mr. Harrington folded his lanky legs, bent at the waist, then, with unexpected grace, ducked beneath the door. From the dim inside, he called to me with a voice sharpened to a cold, fine point, "Well, are you coming or not?" I felt a tiny jab in my chest with each precisely pronounced word. It brought back the memory of the humiliation I'd felt when Joey B. stabbed me with his pencil in second grade and the teacher said I deserved it.

"I'm coming!" I squeaked, bit my bottom lip to stop its trembling and moved down the length of the garage. I scrambled under the door at a distance I estimated would protect me from popping up anywhere near enough to risk making physical contact with Harrington. I cringed at the thought of the mortician's touch; imagined the scent on his dry, crinkled hands; the stench of formaldehyde blended with the saccharin sweetness of roses.

Inside, I squinted and peered around shadows. Why had he brought me here? I looked around for clues. No parked vehicles. A bucket and mop holed up in a corner; a misplaced bag forgotten in the middle of the oil-stained cement floor.

The dim light hovering beneath the half-opened door so illuminated Mr. Harrington that he appeared almost to glide across the greasy floor to the lone bag. Watching me, he bent down and unzipped its top. The metal teeth disengaged with reluctance and expressed their fury with metallic gnashing that surfed the sound waves trapped within the garage, setting my ears to jangling, my composure teetering. The corners of the mortician's lips turned up slightly into something that resembled a smile. For a brief moment my distaste for the man turned to pity.

The undertaker tucked his smile away, stood and began speaking in a matter-of-fact tone that didn't match the occasion or his words. If you'd happened upon us, you'd have thought he was talking about nothing more unsettling than the weather. "They pulled her out of the Muskingum Sunday morning. A guy out fishing spotted her and called it in. They know she wasn't no jumper since they found her upstream above the bridge. Darn lucky too! Might've been weeks before she'd popped up if she'd gotten pulled down beneath that dam."

He paused and looked directly at me to make sure I was taking this all in. He continued, becoming more animated, talking with his hands, enjoying the telling, "Found her just below Armco Steel, snagged on some high-water trash washed downstream after all that rain they'd had up north a few weeks back. Said she'd probably been in the water a day or two. Not sure exactly how she ended up in the drink, but the coroner wrote it off as a suicide after talking to your boss and her daddy. Her daddy's sending somebody down to pick her up later. We got to verify the ID before we release her. Your boss said you knew her. One of them problem girls, huh? Must've been some kind of crazy! That her?" He stepped back; twisted his head toward the bag.

I walked slowly to the bag and stood without looking down. I felt his arrogance crawling like a tick up my neck and the mean, unwavering pressure of his stare threatened to topple me. I widened my stance, steadied my center of gravity. He knew I wasn't cut out for this; he waited patiently; a judge anxious to rate my response.

I braced myself and looked just long enough to reconcile memory with reality. "Her name was *Anna*," I whispered, only to release my friend—not this thing that I did not know—from this sordid inspection and the indignity of the place. The girl I'd known had suffered enough; I'd not add a display of my sorrow to the rocks already piled upon her soul. The mortician could be dammed. I'd not squander my tears for Anna on him.

Refusing to give Harrington so much as another glance, I slipped again beneath the garage door. Awash in sunshine and fresh air, I ran to my car, climbed in, bent over the steering wheel, and began sobbing and gulping air like I'd been gut-punched. When I could breathe again, I fumbled for my keys and started the car.

Backing slowly out of the parking space, I was startled when I saw my image in the rearview mirror. I swiped away tears and snot with the back of my hand, expecting to adjust my reflection, but it was unwavering. With the exception of the two slight vertical creases now furrowing the previously smooth skin between my brows, the contours of my face, the tear-blotched skin, and the dark roots of my grown-out hair said, yes, it's *me*. But the eyes disagreed; the reflected eyes were foreign to my face. These eyes were darker, more opaque, hiding knowledge I had not sought. In the same way that what I'd seen in the garage was no longer the Anna I'd known, I understood that the girl, sitting at the wheel of my old Ford and wearing my familiar nurse's whites, was now an altered version of the former me.

* * *

I don't recall the drive back until I was pulling into my assigned parking space. I sat with the car idling for a few minutes and considered going home. I'd call Mr. Hahn and resign, or at least take a few sick days. I got to thinking about starting over somewhere new; I never planned to stay here forever. I could move on or go back to school, bury this day beneath a new life.

I mulled over my options, all the while knowing that the stain had already set; this day was not one to be lived so much as endured. Still, I lingered in the car, avoiding the inevitable by taking my own pulse and counting my respirations. Convinced that my vital signs were stable and unable to think of another excuse to stay inside the car, I shut off the engine, got out, walked to the building, and slipped inside.

My rubber-soled shoes kicked up squeaks and sent them skittering down the empty linoleum hallway. I thought about taking off my shoes and tiptoeing, but before I could make up my mind, I was at the clinic door, relieved that no one had noticed my return.

I leaned against the doorframe and tried to control my shaking hands long enough to unlock the door. When it finally gave way, I jerked the ridiculous clock face sign from its nail, let myself in, crossed the clinic to my desk, and fell into my ugly chair. I swiveled and idly twirled the plastic clock hands, the motion soothing as I concentrated on hardening my mind to steel.

My curious colleagues would show up soon enough, entering like a solemn troop of thespians auditioning for a Greek tragedy, concern plastered like greasepaint to their faces. They'd do their best to coerce from me the most tantalizingly morbid details of my morning. But I would be ready; I'd not forsake Anna. I composed my new face and waited.

The Bull, the China

He put a hole in the wall, but it was a small hole.
He shaved his head when he lost a bet, but hair grows back.
The bumper was dented, but Jimmy popped it out again.
The vase broke, but there was always another,
an empty moonshine jar, a green wine bottle.
The basketball was stabbed, but its twin stepped in.
The video game smashed with a hammer was easily forgotten.
The meat went rancid, so we conjured a pizza.
He bruised her arm, but brought a kitten home, something even
    weaker.
My brother's dented ribs were golden again in a week.
The kicked dog bounded back, happy to see another morning.
He drove into the hydrangeas. They bloomed again next spring.
The table poxed with burns was easy to paint clean.
Was I the only thing shot through with cracks for which there was
    no glue?

Season of Harvest

Leaves the color of copper pennies
hang on the oaks
outside our windows.
Your heart heavy with grief
over your father's mid-October death.

All that was
but also
all that wasn't
for so many reasons.

The hills around us colored blood-red,
corn-yellow, and sunset-orange.
In this season of harvest,
you'd like to have more to lose.

Seasons of Chico

Through the kitchen window, no person or beast peered back, so he went outside. The air was still and close, a proper day to die. At first, he knew. Dementia had tapped him on his shoulder not long after his Belva died. She had always handled everything about their modest affairs, the bills, checkbook, insurance. Groceries. He was just making a shit mess of it all. Had even forgotten that he figured out it was dementia. Was only aware of the crippling confusion, terrified by it.

He lit a Winston and watched his exhale battle the weight of the air, finally succumbing to dispersion, vanishing. His aging bird dog, Chico, gazed at the smoke too, but mostly he just watched the old man, waiting for clues. The man wiped sweat from his forehead. A forehead wrinkled and splotched with seventy years of hard farming in an unrepentant sun.

Yet it was Belva whom skin cancer chose to claim, barging into their sweet existence, violating her precious porcelain skin, scampering off into the darkness like a hyena, with the hopes for their fading years in its teeth.

Chico led the way as they strolled out to the weathered red barn. The intent had been to close the barn door; a task neglected the night before. By the time they reached it, the old farmer wondered why they had ambled that far from the house.

"What, honey?" The man responded to no one, hand cupping his ear toward an owl up deep in the dark rafters.

Inside the barn, it was hot as a two-peckered goat, as he used to like to say. Hard to breathe. Seemed to be getting more and more scorching, like the world's thermostat had flaked out. The morning sun lit up the infinite particulate matter cloaking the air. Chico sat down and searched the man's face for a tell, some hint as to what was up. The dog was searching quite a bit these days.

In the fall of the year, they would always hunt the fencerows, flushing the occasional pheasant or rabbit. Chico loved the hunt, the chilled air, the scent of game, the excitement of the shot, and the pats on the head. Then the warm fireplace and the sweet, deep naps on the rug. But it was so steamy this day. So odd to Chico.

Under a mildewed canvas tarp in the barn rested the vintage half-ton Ford pickup in which the old man had dated Belva. For good measure, they pre-consummated their eventual marriage in the cargo bed under the fireworks of a long-ago July. Just to be sure. Got a good twenty years of service out of the truck before draping it with the tarp. He knew he could never get rid of the thing. An executor would have to deal with it, one day. What he did not know was that his current truck sat quiet on the cinder driveway with the keys in the ignition. He had forgotten to kill the engine the night prior, when he returned from someplace he couldn't recall. Its tank ran dry, like the old man's well of memories.

Chico wagged his cropped tail in a pensive beat. A few tick scars showed through his fur. The old man made his way past the rusting corn heads to the back of the barn, where, in a small office, a gun safe held some shotguns. It was unlocked, the door cracked open. He had been either too trusting or too careless. He reached into the safe and lifted out an old Fulton Special double-barreled 12 gauge, its checkered walnut stock scratched by years of briars.

Chico wiggled with a bit more energy, though he was confused. He knew the fencerows were yet full, thriving with weeds and thick turgid leaves. It was always colder when they hunted, the weeds having died off and the leaves either curled or fallen. The apples from the tree, too. They were always on the ground, rotting and smelling so sweet when they hunted. But they were still up in the tree, too long it seemed, sagging the branches. Like fishing poles weighted by big-mouth bass from the pond, where Chico chased frogs.

Chico knew the seasons. The rhythms of his world. At least he thought he did. Things new, things old. Some born as others died. Seasons did not usually negotiate. He looked up at the old man's face. He had just removed a box of shotgun shells from the top shelf of the safe. He fumbled a bit, but managed to load both barrels of the shotgun, then snap it shut. Usually, he dropped a few extra rounds into his pocket. This time he did not.

Chico picked up on the clues. A hunt was imminent. He was thrilled, if still perplexed. So very hot, it seemed, to hunt. But he was game. Ready for the pursuit.

"Come Chico," the old man said. "Wanna' hunt?"

Chico spun a few circles and yipped.

Through the thick weeds and grasses, they trudged, Chico weaving as best he could amidst the heavy growth, scenting as he went.

"Find 'em boy," the old man coached.

Chico was already panting as he labored through the heartless heat and gnarly foliage. Sweat crept its way into the old man's eyes. He paused to rub. Soon, they turned course and were hunting the ditch next to the paved main road. This confused Chico further. They had never hunted along the road before. A car filled both front and back with a wide-eyed family, staring at the pair, sped by, tires humming.

The old man then crossed the road, wading into a soybean field, one that belonged to a neighboring farm. Chico hesitated. He had never been allowed to cross the road. He did not know these new lands. A whine, then a nervous yip of questioning, followed.

"Come on, boy," the old man ordered. "Hunt 'em up!"

Assured by the tone of the man's voice, Chico padded across the road, the heat from the asphalt a new and unpleasant sensation. Into the beans he leapt, resuming his sniffing for signs of game. Several hundred yards into the soybeans, which were stressed from the heat, the old man stopped. He was soaked. His mouth sagged. Humidity hung in a low-slung opaque cloud. Chico kept hunting, weaving, and jumping, panting through the beans. Soon he broke through, into a clearing ten yards from the man.

Chico was not sure what to make of the posture of the old man. He appeared to be in the position he would assume prior to shooting at a bird or rabbit; only Chico had not pointed any game. The man also had never leveled the loud noisemaker in his direction before. Chico froze, unsure what to do.

The old man looked down the barrel of the shotgun, which had begun to quiver, shake even.

Chico cocked his head, trying to decipher the sounds uttered by the man. To translate them into some sensible action. But they were only whimpers, not the usual curt hunting commands.

Haltingly, the old man lowered the shotgun, his body quaking.

"Belva!" he cried out, ending their odd moment of communion in the clearing.

Over and over, he called for his deceased wife.

Chico's nubby tail twitched. Belva was a name that warmed him inside out. He had not heard it for some time now, though he faithfully listened. He loved greeting Belva in the cinder driveway when she returned from the grocery store, yipping and circling her as she toted the bags inside. Once the bags were emptied, Belva would give him a crunchy treat from the cupboard and massage his head. She would let Chico doze on the bed, only for the old man to awaken and push him back off.

"Belva!" The old man yelled again. "Oh, Jesus. I'm lost. Belva!"

Hearing the repeated calls to Belva was a symphony to Chico's ears. In a rare flash of disobedient selfishness, Chico began to bolt back to their farm. Toward the cinder driveway, hurtling over the sickly soybean plants two at a time. His sweet, sweet Belva.

As Chico's feet hit the pavement of the road, a single blast from the shotgun roared across the massive field like a thunderous rebuke from God.

Chico halted. In normal times he would bolt to retrieve the fallen pheasant or the rabbit. But he had not pointed or chased either prior to the shot. He was so very unsure about this day. Chico scanned the vast field, heart pounding. There was no sign of the old man. Only the acrid scent of spent powder.

Certain to Chico, as he stood there determining his next move, was that his paws were burning, becoming stuck in the broiling asphalt. Yelping, he loped onward, toward that cinder driveway. Relieved by the sweet lushness of the damp cool grasses. On he ran, his eager eyes gleaned through the growing haze. Seeking a first glimpse of his Belva.

Old Hearts

When he felt the wave of restrained exuberance explode
from the nearby schoolhouse, the old man righted the topsy rabbit
dangling calmly in his grasp and folded the buck
into the crook of his arm. With sleight of hand, his knife
    disappeared
into the tool box housed in an empty hutch.

He turned back to two little girls standing in the alley,
their Mary Janes planted in cinders a toe short of his property;
their eyes ferrying love across the wee yard to the caged rabbits.
The man motioned the girls into the lot and resettled the old buck
into its rightful cage. From another hutch, he reached under a doe
and lifted two of the kits clinging to her teats.

The little girls plopped crisscross in the unkept grass, biting
their lower lips in concentration, absorbing the old man's
    gentleness,
like a dab of their mother's night cream, into their own hands.
He passed a yawning kit to each child. The girls hummed breathy
lullabies into the bunnies' flower-bud ears, smiled when a tiny heart
fluttered against a palm.

The children's mother noticed their tardiness and called them
home to dinner. The girls kissed their bunnies and handed them,
like delicate pysanky, to the old man. As they ran down the alley,
he nestled the kits against the doe, his callused fingers directed
their sucking mouths to the wellspring of their desire.

Again, the man lifted the old buck from its cage, scratched its ears

and held it to his chest until both old hearts slowed to a
    harmonized beat.
He kissed the rabbit's head, reached for his tool box
and carried his old friend to the back of the shed.

Amëwei Shukël: Bee Sugar

I have never been a beekeeper, but I have been a gardener and a keeper of pets. I have raised one child, and taught many more, so I know how to be responsible and loving, caring, and consciously disciplined. Several weeks ago, I was reading my great-great grandmother's obituary, and I discovered she had been a beekeeper. Two years prior to her death, she had harvested 1,000 pounds of honey. I tried to imagine this harvest, and I realized how little I knew about bees and their lives, so I began reading about them. I learned about the power of the queen bee, and, from that, I understood something differently about the women in my family. Of course, we do not kill our husbands, but we are generally treated as royalty by them. We know how to work, and often not only instigate endless improvement projects, but assist with the work required, turning ideas into reality.

My ancestors, John and Mary Swaggart Witherite, married on February 20, 1845. Between 1845 and 1865, Mary bore five children: Martha, Alfred, Mary, Michael, and Clara. John worked two jobs: one in the coal mines, and the other chopping wood to earn enough money to leave the mines and become a farmer. He purchased ninety-four acres from the Lenni Lenape. On that land, two years before Mary died in 1891, she harvested 1,000 pounds of honey.

I try to imagine the exchange between the Lenni Lenape and my ancestors as land was bought and sold. My European ancestors surveyed the land and took the survey to the land office where the deed was written and recorded. I have a worn copy of the deed in a metal box, but no one in my family has claim to the property now. The Witherites cleared their unbroken land, working at night by firelight to make the land ready for planting while they simultaneously built their cabin.

I wonder what the Lenni Lenape, a nomadic group who were known as part of the Northeastern Nation, thought of these pale-skinned, light-eyed Europeans. The land being purchased had been part of the larger Algonquin tribes' shared hunting ground for centuries.

In 1845, John and Mary owned a bed and borrowed a skillet to start housekeeping. They had no chairs, no knives, no forks, her obituary tells us. For the first eight years of their marriage, they lived in a small cabin, and did not build their house until eight years later in 1853. When they built it, they made sure part of it stood over Wild Cat Creek's waters, so they could benefit from the natural refrigeration.

Mary's obituary claims that "she had more than ordinary business capacity, that she managed her farm with excellent skill, and that she displayed sound judgment and applied careful consideration in all her decisions." She became interested in bee culture and honey when she was a child, and she maintained that interest for her entire life. As an adult, she kept fifty hives, collecting what the Lenape call amëwei shukël—bee sugar. This was an art for her and a form of prayer.

Her beekeeping gave her the opportunity to practice daily-ness, intentionality, and mindfulness while demonstrating her respect for nature. I imagine the glass jars sitting on her pantry windowsill, the sunlight passing through, illuminating the room with golden light.

* * *

Soon after reading her obituary, I began to dream about honey, and on my walks in the countryside, I heard buzzing. In my spare time, I read about bees. I reflected on the fact that sterile female bees make a half teaspoon of honey in their lifetime of approximately six to eight weeks. How many half teaspoons are there in a sixteen-ounce jar? I researched this and learned the answer: one hundred and ninety-two. That means one jar represents the fruit of the labor of one hundred and ninety-two bees. That means 1,000 pounds of honey, the amount Mary Swaggart Witherite harvested two years before her death, redeemed the work of one hundred ninety-two thousand bees. Let that sink in.

What measure did my great-great grandmother bring to bear on herself and the work she did in a day, a week, a month, a year, a decade? What measure can I bring to measure my life with any clarity? How many poems have I written? How many stories have I told? How many books have I imagined, and how many of these did I complete? How many have I destroyed?

Instead of keeping bees, I taught and administered in schools in four states from pre-school to college over a forty-year period. I have been married for forty years and raised one child. How can I measure my rate of success? Do I consult with my husband? Do I send a survey to my daughter?

* * *

The first documentation of humans gathering honey 8,000 years ago is preserved in cave paintings in Cuevas de la Arana, España. The paintings show a person holding onto a liana, a long-stemmed vine, while swinging near the hive. Bees encircle the gatherer, and the person scoops honeycomb. In many cultures, honey is god food, used to celebrate beginnings, endings, and everything in between. Some cultures buried honey with their dead. The honey was made from linden berries, and meadow flowers. The intent? To help their loved ones journey safely until they connected with a greater spirit.

Many religious sources refer to bees and honey. Buddha retreated to the wilderness to find peace and inhabit it. When he became hungry, a monkey brought him honey to eat, to restore his energy and his spirit. The Hebrew people use honey, and always have, to celebrate the arrival of the new and the hope it holds for the future.

John the Baptist believed the bee was close to God and that God was close to the bee. While wandering in the desert, John the Baptist ate a diet of locusts and honey. He believed eating honey would bring him closer to God. He believed that through his preaching, he would bring the people of Israel closer to God. He succeeded. His unusual diet brought him visions, and his visions informed and inspired those who heard him speak.

The bee is close to God; and God is close to the bee. Both are pure sweetness, some people think. Pure nourishment for body and soul.

* * *

I have been writing long past midnight. Light is streaking across the eastern sky—a frail yellow sunrise, accented with a line or two of peach. I make a cup of coffee, put on my jean jacket, and leave a note on the counter for my husband: "I've gone to Pennsylvania." He'll know where and why.

I take the old roads. I head south through Pennsylvania's wilds. I see mountain laurel, sycamore trees, bear cubs, some well-maintained homes with border gardens of forget-me-nots, some poorly maintained properties, the lawns filled with rusting cars and junk. I listen for the buzzing of bees leading me home to Wild Cat Holler, where my great-great grandmother kept her beehives and caught fish with her bare hands in Wild Cat Creek.

Ephemera

Mayapples speak
in turtle,
wrapping seeds

in sweetness
ripening
in turtle time;

the speckled
nectar
of *Claytonia*

(spring beauty)
sings
just a moment

above the soil,
its fairy spuds
shaping

a long
fermata
underground.

Crossroads

The Muse is the doe
in the road you miss
hitting, the one crossing
on cautious hooves,
sniffing the air
for your secrets.
On the other side,
she turns back, gazing
with a curious gleam
as if asking what you
mean if not danger.
Now she's leaping
off with a flick
of white tail you take
as invitation.
You may follow
her through mist
between the trees,
beside the marsh or stream,
through the bright
and dull seasons of wings.
All she asks is that
you forget your car,
your destination, and every
map you've ever believed in.

Andrew Vogel

Bear

Now that the weekenders have all
cleared out and the branch has gone
quiet, I keep expecting to see that old
mother bear lumbering down off
Middle Hill, flabby in her appetites,
sniffing for salt, mad to lick a spill
of butter from the stones of one
of these ramshackle fire rings.
Everyone has a story of seeing her
that they tell over and over again.

The barking crows, I am sure, are
following her, pesky harbingers.
I scan the shelf of light that cuts
into the trees as far as I can see
and listen with all my posture.
The juncos and quick chipmunks
fussing in the leaf litter lift the
hair of my neck. A windfall stick
hits the ground, and I flinch.
It's only a breeze moving through
the wildflowers across the creek,
but every shirr in the trees must be
her, stalking, chuffing, salivating.

From valley floor to high knob,
pine grove to escarpment, she plods
every lobe of the watershed, squelching
her way through the mud of an upland

spring, splashing through muck wallows,
flipping downs for grubs. Patient and fast
as the lapping seasons, she attends the
implacable honesty of the backwoods,
pungent in her sleep under a sill of rock,
harried by mosquitos as she walks, quiet,
oily as smoke, drawing every scent from
bocage to piedmont into the grain of her
mind, even us, all the junk, all the smut.

CONTRIBUTOR BIOS

Rachel Allen
Rachel Allen lives in Johnstown, Pa. She teaches yoga to survivors of sexual assault and domestic violence in community-based settings and plays Celtic Harp in hospice. Her writing is featured in *Hags on Fire*, *Northern Appalachia Review* and Long Shot Books and *Christians Practicing Yoga Blog*. Rachel's chapbook "Blessings Beyond Bypass" is slated for publication in July of 2022.

Valerie Bacharach
Valerie Bacharach's writing has appeared or will appear in: *The Ekphrastic Review*, *Vox Populi*, *Whale Road Review*, *The Blue Mountain Review*, *EcoTheo Review*, *Kosmos Quarterly Journal*, *Amethyst Review*, *On the Seawall*, *Poetica*, *Minyon Magazine*, *One Art*, and *Writer's Foundry Review*. She has two published chapbooks and has been nominated twice for a Pushcart Prize.

Jillian Barnet
Jillian Barnet writes poetry and nonfiction exploring loss, identity, and the ways experiences reverberate, sometimes for generations. Her work has appeared in *New Letters*, *North American Review*, *Nimrod*, *Image*, and elsewhere. Her chapbook, "Falling Bodies" is available through Finishing Line Press. She recently relocated to a tiny farm in the Finger Lakes where she is working on a memoir.

Roy Bentley
A finalist for the Miller Williams prize, Roy Bentley has published ten books of poetry. His work has appeared in *Shenandoah*, *Blackbird*, *North American Review*, *Crazyhorse*, *The Southern Review*, and *Prairie Schooner* among others. His latest collection, *Beautiful Plenty*, is available from Main Street Rag.

Betsy Bolton

Betsy Bolton's work has appeared in *Coldnoon* and *The Poet's Attic.* "Worm sex" is forthcoming in *The Hopper: Environmental Lit. Poetry. Art.* She teaches at Swarthmore College, on Lenape land, at the edge of the Piedmont and the coastal plain.

Joel Burcat

Joel Burcat is the author of: *Drink to Every Beast; Amid Rage;* and *Strange Fire.* An environmental lawyer, he edited non-fiction books on environmental law. His story, "Something Terrible and Beautiful," set in 1944, was published in volume 3 of *Northern Appalachia Review*, and is a prequel both to *Strange Fire* and his short story, "Strange Fire: The Movie."

Jack Burgess

Jack Burgess has been a soldier, teacher, union officer, and labor relations consultant. He has degrees from Ohio State in history and political science, English literature and composition. His chapbook is titled *It's Always Gettysburg.* His columns on government and politics appear in *The Chillicothe Gazette* and online. His poetry is intentionally accessible.

William Burtch

William Burtch is co-author of *W.G.* (Sunbury Press) and has been a finalist for the American Fiction Short Story Award (New Rivers Press). Recent work has been published or is forthcoming in *Great Lakes Review, Gone Lawn, Ruminate Magazine, Schuylkill Valley Journal* and *Alive in the World Vol 3,* (Riverfeet Press). He has lived in or around Northern Appalachia most of his life. He tweets at @WilliamBurtch2. More at williamburtch.com

James Cochran

James Cochran is a proudly Appalachian writer, transplanted from the soil of Southeastern Ohio to the hilly streets of Charleston, West Virginia. He embraces the practice of mindfulness through writing, and writing through mindfulness, and enjoys listening to the neighbor's wind chimes.

Noah Davis

Noah Davis grew up in Tipton, Pennsylvania, and writes about the Allegheny Front. Davis's poetry collection *Of This River* was selected for the 2019 Wheelbarrow Emerging Poet Book Prize from Michigan State University's Center for Poetry, and his poems and prose have appeared in *The Sun, Southern Humanities Review, Best New Poets*, and *Orion* among others. His work has been nominated for the Pushcart Prize and awarded a Katharine Bakeless Nason Fellowship at the Bread Loaf Writers Conference and the 2018 Jean Ritchie Appalachian Literature Fellowship from Lincoln Memorial University.

Todd Davis

Todd Davis is the author of seven full-length collections of poetry, most recently *Coffin Honey* and *Native Species*, both published by Michigan State University Press. He has won the Foreword INDIES Book of the Year Bronze and Silver Awards, the Gwendolyn Brooks Poetry Prize, the Chautauqua Editors Prize, and the Bloomsburg University Book Prize. He teaches environmental studies at Pennsylvania State University's Altoona College.

Laura Dennis

Laura Dennis is a language professor and writer-in-progress at a college in Kentucky. Her creative nonfiction has been published in *MER Vox Quarterly, Bethlehem Writers Roundtable, Change Seven*, and *Bluff & Vine*. When she is not teaching or writing, she enjoys music, reading, and spending time with her friends, family, and pets.

Dana A. Dever

Dana A. Dever, a product of higher education laid over a Southern blue-collar pedigree, has a heritage grounded in the hill country of Kentucky. Kayaking Appalachian rivers for years, he gained a unique perspective of what was and what is now. Poetry is his means of dealing with a world of inanity, counter-balanced by moments of beauty and clarity.

Tom Donlon

Tom Donlon lives with his wife and children in Shenandoah Junction, WV. He earned an MFA in Creative Writing from the American University in Washington, DC, before moving to West Virginia in 1986. He was awarded a chapbook, *Peregrine*, in November 2016 from a book contest sponsored by the Franciscan University in Steubenville, OH. Poems have appeared in many journals, newspapers, and anthologies. Recognition has included Pushcart Prize nominations and a fellowship from the WV Commission on the Arts.

Charlene Fix

Charlene Fix, mother of three, grandmother of two, is an Emeritus English Prof. at Columbus College of Art & Design. Her poetry collections are *Taking a Walk in My Animal Hat* (Bottom Dog), *Frankenstein's Flowers* (CW Books), *Flowering Bruno* (XOXOX), and *Jewgirl* (forthcoming, Eyewear), her prose homage *Harpo Marx as Trickster* (McFarland). Charlene co-coordinates Hospital Poets at OSU. Her website: Charlenefix.com.

Daniel Flatley

Daniel Flatley participated in many theater productions in his home-town of Wheeling, W.Va., before enlisting in the Marine Corps in 2004. After leaving the military, he studied English Literature and Journalism at Columbia University in the City of New York, where he also indulged a passion for the performing arts before becoming a reporter. He now works in Washington, D.C., and lives in Maryland with his wife and two children.

Kenneth Gournic

Kenneth Gournic spent his last dozen years in the Pittsburgh Division of the United States Postal Inspection Service. He worked several fraud cases in the Northern District of West Virginia at the U. S. Attorney's offices in Wheeling, Clarksburg, and Martinsburg. The people and places he came in contact with made up some of the best experiences of his professional life. Gournic retired from that position after 36 years, then enrolled in the Writing Certificate Program at the University of Pittsburgh. That experience was so enjoyable for him; the doing of it, regardless of success or failure, was worth every single moment spent.

Richard Hague

Richard Hague, Artist-in-Residence at Thomas More University, is author or editor of 20 volumes. He has work recently in *Cutthroat: A Journal of the Arts* and in the anthology *Wild Gods!: The Ecstatic in Contemporary American Poetry and Prose* from New Rivers Press. He is 2021-22 President of the Literary Club of Cincinnati.

Lisa Harris

Lisa Harris, MFA, is from the Allegheny Mountains of Central Pennsylvania. Her publications include three novels: *'Geechee Girls, Allegheny Dream,* and *The Raven's Tale,* (Ravenna Press) and four poetry collections, *Traveling Through Glass, Dwelling Space,* (Cayuga Lake Books) *Broken Open,* and *Carry Light, Carry Fire* (Wasteland Press). Her fiction has received two first prizes from Bright Hill Press, been nominated for inclusion in Best Short Stories, and included in a variety of anthologies.

Kirk Judd

Kirk Judd has lived, worked, trout fished and wandered around in West Virginia all of his life. Kirk was a member of the Appalachian Literary League, a founding member and former president of West Virginia Writers, Inc. and is a founding member and creative writing instructor for Allegheny Echoes, Inc.

Kip Knott

Kip Knott spent whole summers of his childhood living with his grandparents in the coal mining ghost town of Hemlock, Ohio. His most recent full-length book of poetry, *Clean Coal Burn,* is available from Kelsay Books. His first collection of short stories, *Some Birds Nest in Broken Branches,* is available from Alien Buddha Press.

Jack Kogut

Jack Kogut is a native of Martins Ferry, Ohio and a mostly amateur writer of mostly fiction. His work has recently appeared in *Planisphere Q: Fire and Ice* and *Phantom Kangaroo* and not so recently in *The Washington Post* and *Omni* magazine. He works as a scientist in aerospace research and development and lives with his family in Maryland.

Sandra Kolankiewicz

Most recently, Sandra Kolankiewicz's poems have appeared in *Fortnightly Review, Galway Review, The Healing Muse, New World Writing,* and *Appalachian Review.* She is the author of *Turning Inside Out, The Way You Will Go,* and *Lost in Transition.*

Donna J. Long

Donna J. Long is Professor of English at Fairmont State University in Fairmont, WV, and Editor of *Kestrel: A Journal of Literature and Art.* Her poems have appeared in many journals, including *Canary, The Southern Review, Clockhouse,* and *Kindred.*

Jessica Manack

Jessica Manack holds degrees from Hollins University and lives with her family in Pittsburgh, Pennsylvania. Her writing has recently appeared in *San Pedro River Review, Black Fork Review,* and *The Pittsburgh Post-Gazette.*

Matthew Martello

Matthew Martello was born and raised in Steubenville, Ohio. He graduated from The Ohio State University in 2018 and is currently a doctoral candidate in English Literature at the University of Virginia, where he teaches and researches British and American poetry from the late eighteenth century to the present. His academic writing has appeared or is forthcoming in *Narrative* and *Blake/An Illustrated Quarterly.*

Dennis McFadden

Dennis McFadden lives and writes in a cedar-shingled cottage called Summerhill in the woods of upstate New York. His collection *Jimtown Road* won the Press 53 Award for Short Fiction; his stories have appeared in dozens of publications including *The Missouri Review, New England Review, The Sewanee Review, Crazyhorse, The Antioch Review, The Massachusetts Review* and *Best American Mystery Stories.*

annie mcwilliams

annie mcwilliams, born in Martins Ferry, Ohio, is a retired nurse, an environmental activist, and a descendant of over twenty Revolutionary War Patriots. An outsider writer, she is a member of Ohio Poetry Association and has been published in *Common Threads, Spring Street, Northern Appalachia Review*, and multiple annual Ohio Poetry Day Association's *Best Of* anthologies.

Beth Meko

Beth Meko is originally from north central West Virginia and currently lives in Knoxville, Tennessee, where she is a grant writer and university lecturer. Her short fiction has appeared in the *Anthology of Appalachian Writers, Longleaf Review, Valparaiso Fiction Review, Wilderness House Literary Review, Blue Lake Review*, and *Still: The Journal*, and is forthcoming in *Oyster River Pages*.

Ben Moyer

Ben Moyer writes about nature, outdoors, and conservation issues from his home in western Pennsylvania. He is a winner of the Outdoor Writers Association of America Excellence in Craft lifetime award, two Golden Quill awards from the Western Pennsylvania Press Club, and numerous other honors. His work appears in numerous state, regional, and national publications.

Deni Naffziger

Deni Naffziger was raised in Ohio's Appalachian Steel Valley but has lived in Athens, Ohio for over 30 years. Her work has appeared in *New Ohio Review, Atticus Review, Pine Mountain Sand & Gravel, Pikeville Review,* and elsewhere. Her first book of poems, *Desire to Stay*, was published in 2014. Her second book, *Strange Bodies*, will be published by Shadelandhouse Modern Press in 2023.

Karen Whittington Nelson

Karen Whittington Nelson writes poetry and fiction from her home on a small Southeastern Ohio farm. Her work has been published in the anthology, *I Thought I Heard a Cardinal Sing: Ohio's Appalachian Voices, Sheila-Na-Gig Online, Northern Appalachia Review, Women of Appalachia Project's Women Speak Volumes 2–7, Anthology of Appalachian Writers, Gyroscope Review,* and *Pudding Magazine: The Journal of Applied Poetry.*

Virginia Parfitt

Virginia Parfitt was born and raised in western Pennsylvania. Much of her writing is informed by the rural landscape of northern Appalachia, the sounds and the scents, and the life and the death of the Earth. She nourishes these passions with words, written and spoken. An emerging poet and writer, she uses words to make sense of her world, with the intention that her words may help you make sense of your world, too. She resides and writes in southeastern Pennsylvania with her family.

Joshua Penrod

Joshua Penrod is a native of Johnstown, Pennsylvania, and he still makes his home in that part of Northern Appalachia. He works for an international organization based in Washington, DC, representing a specialized area of the biomedical products industry. He holds a PhD from Virginia Tech and is also an adjunct professor at the Merrick School of Business at the University of Baltimore.

David B. Prather

David B. Prather is the author of *We Were Birds*. His work has appeared in many journals, including *Poet Lore, Prairie Schooner, Seneca Review*, and others. He studied acting at the National Shakespeare Conservatory, and he studied writing at Warren Wilson College. He lives in Parkersburg, WV.

Judith Rosenberg

Judith Rosenberg has a PhD, Brandeis University, MA Indiana University, BA Boston University. Assistant Professor of English, she has taught at Hunter College (NYC), University of Massachusetts (Boston), and L'Institut Catholique de Paris. She currently resides in New York City where she conducts a workshop for publishing poets.

Alberto Ríos selected her poem "Venetian Passageway" for Honorable Mention published in *The MacGuffin's Poet Hunt Contest, Winter 2019*. In an earlier issue of that journal Gerald Stern awarded Honorable Mention to "When the Man You Love Lies." Her poems have also appeared in *Crosswinds, The Atlanta Review* (International Competition Finalist), *The Antigonish Review, The Louisville Review, Paterson Literary Review*.

Larry Smith

Larry Smith is a native of the industrial Ohio Valley and a professor emeritus of Bowling Green State University in Ohio. A poet, fiction writer, and critic, he is the editor and publisher of Bottom Dog Press and its Appalachian Writing Series.

Judith Sornberger

Judith Sornberger's full-length poetry collections are: *Angel Chimes: Poems of Advent and Christmas* (Shanti Arts, 2020), *I Call to You from Time* (Wipf & Stock, 2019), *Practicing the World* (CavanKerry, 2018) and *Open Heart* (Calyx Books). Her prose memoir *The Accidental Pilgrim: Finding God and His Mother in Tuscany* is from Shanti Arts. She lives on the side of a mountain outside Wellsboro, PA. www.judithsornberger.net.

Lois Spencer

Lois Spencer's short stories have recently appeared in *Women Speak, The Poorhouse Rag, Change Seven,* and *Northern Appalachia Review.* Persimmon Tree has accepted a story for its summer issue. A short story collection, *To Tell the Truth,* will soon join her 2017 memoir, *In the Language of My Country.* Lois formerly taught English in Southeastern Ohio.

Jacob Strautmann

Jacob Strautmann's collection *The Land of the Dead Is Open for Business* is available from Four Way Books as will be the forthcoming *New Vrindaban.* Awarded a 2018 Massachusetts Poetry Fellowship by the Massachusetts Cultural Council, Jacob Strautmann's poems have appeared in *The Boston Globe, The Appalachian Journal, Southern Humanities Review* and *Blackbird.* www.jacobstrautmann.com

Thomas Strunk

Thomas Strunk grew up in Minisink Hills, Pennsylvania, on the Delaware River. His work strives to express the longing for spiritual, emotional, and political liberation. His writing has appeared or is forthcoming in *Pinyon, DASH, Anthology of Appalachian Writers,* and *East Fork Journal.* Thomas blogs at LiberationNow.org. He now lives in Northside, Cincinnati with his wife and twin daughters.

Matthew Ussia

Matthew Ussia is a professor, editor, podcaster, thereminist, writer, soft-core punk, social media burnout, and all-around sentient organic matter. His first book of poetry, *The Red Glass Cat,* was published in 2021. His writings have appeared in *Mister Rogers and Philosophy, Trailer Park Quarterly,* and *Anti-Heroin Chic* among others. He lives in Pittsburgh. More info can be found at matthewussia.com.

Andrew Vogel

Andrew Vogel listens, walks the hills, and teaches in rural eastern Pennsylvania, the homelands of the displaced Lenape peoples. His poems have appeared most recently in *Poetry East, Hunger Mountain, Crab Creek Review,* and *The Briar Cliff Review.*

Gabriel Welsch

Gabriel Welsch is the author of a collection of short stories, *Groundscratchers,* and four collections of poems, the latest of which is *The Four Horsepersons of a Disappointing Apocalypse.* He lives in Pittsburgh, Pennsylvania, and works as a vice president for marketing and communications at Duquesne University.

Caroline Wermuth

As outreach coordinator for the Pennsylvania Center for the Book in the Penn State University Libraries, Caroline Wermuth coordinates the Public Poetry Project, Lee Bennett Hopkins Award for Children's Poetry, and Lynd Ward Prize for Graphic Novel. Her poems have appeared in *Northern Appalachia Review, Frogpond, Heron's Nest,* and *World Haiku Review.*

Dick Westheimer

Dick Westheimer has—with his wife and writing companion Debbie— lived on their plot of land in rural southwest Ohio for over 40 years. His most recent poems have appeared or are upcoming in *Rattle, Paterson Review, Pine Mountain Sand and Gravel, RiseUp Review, Minyan, Gyroscope Review,* and *Cutthroat.* More can be found at dickwestheimer.com.

Sherrell Wigal

Sherrell Wigal was born, raised and still lives in West Virginia. She writes from her rock-based road roots, with an eye and ear to women and a heart honed to the spirituality in life. To read Sherrell's poetry is to walk into a place we cannot always predict but is also somehow familiar.

Rania Zuri

Rania Zuri is a junior in high school in Appalachia. She is very passionate about Appalachian literature and Appalachian studies. She is a TEDx Speaker, and has been featured on NBC Today, Fox News, and NBC Nightly News with Lester Holt for her work in improving early childhood literacy in Appalachia.

www.ingramcontent.com/pod-product-compliance
Lightning Source LLC
Chambersburg PA
CBHW022010010726
47494CB00003B/982